CREATIVE THINKING AND
PROBLEM SOLVING FOR YOUNG LEARNERS

GIFTED TREASURY SERIES

Jerry D. Flack, Series Editor

CREATIVE THINKING AND PROBLEM SOLVING FOR YOUNG LEARNERS

Karen S. Meador

Illustrated by
Christopher M. Herren

1997
Teacher Ideas Press
A Division of
Libraries Unlimited, Inc.
Englewood, Colorado

This book is dedicated to Don B. Meador.
Your wisdom, creativity, and gentleness guided a teenager
to become a woman. Your love and nurturance
is imperative in my life.

TEACHER IDEAS PRESS
A Division of
Libraries Unlimited, Inc.
P.O. Box 6633
Englewood, CO 80155-6633
1-800-237-6124
www.lu.com/tip

Production Editor: Kay Mariea
Copy Editor: Louise Tonneson
Proofreader: Susie Sigman
Indexer: Lee E. Brower
Design and Layout: Pamela J. Getchell

Library of Congress Cataloging-in-Publication Data

Meador, Karen S., 1949-
    Creative thinking and problem solving for young learners / Karen S. Meador ; illustrated by Christopher M. Herren.
       xxi, 157 p. 22x28 cm. -- (Gifted treasury series)
       Includes bibliographical references.
       ISBN 1-56308-529-1 (pbk.)
       1. Creative thinking--Study and teaching (Elementary)--United States. 2. Problem solving--Study and teaching (Elementary)--United States. 3. Children's literature--Study and teaching (Elementary)--United States.   I. Title.   II. Series.
    LB1590.5.M43   1997
    370.15'7--dc21   97-33633
                                                                          CIP

CONTENTS

FOREWORD

Creative Thinking and Problem Solving for Young Learners is an important and long-awaited book. Fortunately, Karen Meador is the right person to write such a book. She has long been in touch with the creativity of young children and is a scholar of creativity and problem solving. Teachers, parents, and grandparents especially will find this book an exciting adventure.

The author is thoroughly familiar with children's books and their use in learning creativity and problem-solving skills. While she primarily provides examples from trade books, teachers will find that regular school textbooks can be used in the same ways. Reading, history, geography, and other social science books are especially rich in possibilities. Thirty years ago, I served as creativity consultant to a major publisher of reading books. The editors, authors, illustrators, and graphics people became very enthusiastic and produced new products that exceeded my expectations. Not only the stories themselves, but also the illustrations and the print could be used to teach creativity and problem-solving skills.

Let me give an example from the first reader in the series. The book is entitled *A Duck Is a Duck* and contains a story entitled "What Is It?" It begins with a two-page illustration of four children followed by a dog on their way to school. The children try to get the dog to go back home, but the dog finds something in the bushes. After some time they discover that it is a turtle and talk about all the things that the turtle can do. After considering the alternatives, they decide to put the turtle in a box and take it to school. The children ask the teacher to guess what is in the box. The teacher asks the children to give her some clues. Finally she guesses correctly, and the children unveil their prize. Then, the problem becomes what to do with the turtle. The teacher has the children brainstorm possible solutions. After doing this, they establish a criterion: what the turtle likes to do. They decide to put the turtle into the pool in the park and proceed to do this; they make sure that the turtle could do all the things turtles like to do.

This story teaches not only the problem-solving process, but also beginning reading skills, such as reading or interpreting the illustrations, and a beginning reading vocabulary of 16 words with practice with additional words they had already mastered. The teacher could extend the "what is it?" lesson by placing some commonplace object in a box and having the children guess its contents. Other creative and problem-solving skills can be taught by turning the reading into a creative drama or role-playing exploration. This makes the reading more realistic and reveals other problems and conflicts.

I would like to say a few words about the consequences of these kinds of learning. On the basis of my experience, I can assure you that, if the lessons are skillfully and enthusiastically done, you can count upon the following outcomes:

1. Children will check out more library books and read them. (In some schools children checked out two and three times as many books as before using these methods.)

2. Children will ask more questions of teachers, parents, grandparents, experts, and others.

3. Children will become more observant of people, nature, and events in their environment.

4. Children will have more fun learning and like school better.

5. Children will apply the information and skills learned more frequently.

6. Creativity and problem solving will be mastered more thoroughly and meaningfully.

E. Paul Torrance
Athens, Georgia

PREFACE

Creative Thinking and Problem Solving for Young Learners is part of the Gifted Treasury Series edited by Jerry D. Flack. The books in this series provide meaningful information, teaching strategies, and abundant resources for anyone interested in the development of children's potential.

This volume examines creative thinking in students from kindergarten to fourth grade, by providing authentic examples from contemporary classrooms, homes, and libraries. Lessons and other suggestions in the book are based on excellent children's literature selections depicting characters who use creative thinking. *Creative Thinking and Problem Solving for Young Learners* differs from other books containing suggestions for developing creative thinking because the literary characters become models for students.

The purpose of the book is two-fold because it provides lessons adults can use with little preparation and valuable background information that leads toward the depth of understanding needed to develop creative thinking. It is appropriate for teachers, librarians, and also parents, who may want to modify the lessons for use at home.

The development of creative thinking at home and in educational settings is no longer a choice; it is a mandate for survival. This book illustrates how adults may work toward the goal of improving the creative thinking of every child. It answers all of the following questions:

How can children's books be used to facilitate growth in creative thinking?

What are some strategies for writing meaningful activities that facilitate creative thinking?

What are some lessons that allow students to think in new and different ways?

Can not-so-creative teachers facilitate the development of creative thinking skills in children?

What are some quick and easy activities to use with students?

Why is creative thinking important to young children and how can we defend it as good classroom practice? (This is especially relevant to those times when someone walks by the classroom and questions the "fun" going on.)

Life with a creative husband and two creative children gave me "prior experience" before I read my first book about creativity. We were creating all the time, and I didn't even know it! I did wonder about my first-born who, when he was three, wore socks over his ears and spent many mornings as a dog. But, when my second child built elaborate fantasies and went into hysterics when she "left her imaginary friend" at preschool, I knew I needed to learn more about creativity. Reading about creativity helped put these episodes into perspective, and I became hooked. Initially, I wondered how to encourage my own children and my students to be creative, but I was not exactly sure what creative thinking involved.

For the past six years, I have participated in classes, workshops, and seminars on creativity, while reading as much about creativity as possible. Excited after each new learning discovery, I prepared lessons to use with students and experimented with facilitating creativity. Both my thesis and my dissertation in graduate school involved working with children to facilitate creative growth. The more I learn about new educational principles and practices, the more I value creativity.

I believe that teachers love to learn. I am constantly looking for new techniques and materials to keep my teaching fresh and exciting. Isn't that why you are reading this book—because this book is about learning, learning about creativity?

ACKNOWLEDGMENTS

Many children have contributed to this book by teaching the author about learning. They have indicated better ways to approach creative endeavors through their personal involvement in my teaching episodes, demonstrated how to have fun while learning, and certified the value of freely exploring ideas. I am especially indebted to the students at Johnson Elementary School in Southlake, Texas; the kindergarten students in Garland, Texas; and the highly creative students attending the Louisiana Creative Scholars Program.

University undergraduate and graduate students have helped me formulate many ideas found in this book through helpful dialogue and questioning. Their classroom conversations with me have led to many creative "ahas."

I am also indebted to members of the Creativity Division of the National Association for Gifted Students, who have taught me the joy of thinking and acting creatively. There are far too many of these friends to name.

The original artwork by artist Christopher M. Herren gives life to the book. I greatly appreciate the time he siphoned from his painting to originate and create the whimsical fish that so clearly illustrate the creative components. He successfully turned my verbal concepts into visuals.

My family, Don, Brad, and Kim, continue to encourage my writing, and I am thankful to them for their understanding and encouragement. I appreciate their many phone calls to ask how the book was coming, and their positive attitudes regarding my ability to complete this volume.

INTRODUCTION

It's Monday morning in the classroom, and things are not going well. John came to school with a snake in a jar and is telling scary stories about how he got it. Many of the children are petrified, and Sarah is crying loudly. In another part of the room, Matthew and Amy are arguing about who knocked the coats off the coat rack, while Jeremy is quietly hanging them up. Mrs. Jones stands at the door waiting to conference. Yes, she knows she doesn't have an appointment, but this is very important.

What should the teacher do?
Take a deep breath, think fast, and think creatively!

Creative thinking is needed in more areas than art, music, and drama; it is needed for real life. The above episode is an example of an instance when creative thinking could save the day. Children also experience such situations in which they need to solve problems. Additionally, they seek a variety of ways to express themselves and create meaning in their endeavors. The ability to think creatively is essential in life for many reasons, including solving problems, producing meaningful and satisfying ideas and products, and developing works in art forms.

Consider the multiple opportunities that arise during the day to observe creative thinking. Advertisements, especially those shown on television, are perhaps one of the most obvious displays of creative thinking. Television commercials depict analogies that force unusual comparisons, provide unique visual displays developed in a creative mind, and display the results of anthropomorphics (Roukes 1982), in which animals take on human qualities.

Inventions that make life easier also provide concrete examples of novel and appropriate ideas. Cars, microwaves, electric coffee pots, and flush toilets all resulted from the recognition of a need, the use of creative thinking, production of the idea, and acceptance of the product or service by society. Creative thinking results in unusual business combinations, such as the author's personal favorite, a gas station combined with a donut shop, and her husband's favorite, the large hardware stores that house franchised fried chicken establishments.

Look around a school in search of creative thinking. A custodian who maximized a broom handle by taping a yardstick to it used creative thinking to get a soccer ball off the roof. A teacher who covered her head from the rain with old lamination plastic used creative thinking to protect her hair. And, unfortunately, a student who managed to get someone else in trouble, while remaining anonymous, also used creative thinking.

Regrettably, some people erroneously point to other scenarios and products in school as creative. The student who accurately copied a drawing may have demonstrated artistic or technical drawing talent but did not display creative thinking (unless he or she added an original dimension to the picture). A student with a beautiful singing voice may be talented but not, at the same time, creative. Obviously, it is possible for someone to be highly talented and creative; however, we misguide students when we incorrectly label talent as creativity, as it forces some students to believe they cannot think creatively because they do not act, draw, or perform musically.

Knowledge

Students need to realize that gaining knowledge of a subject improves their potential for creative development within it. The vocalist mentioned above may be fundamentally well-prepared to create new music after obtaining an understanding of the elements of music. Students must be willing to devote a great deal of attention to the information or skills required in an area of study, such as music. Children's book illustrators Victoria Chess and Steven Kellogg point out the need for future artists to practice drawing. Chess states, "If you want to be an illustrator, do it all the time and practice, practice, practice" (Cummings 1992, 12). And Kellogg advises, "Get as much practice as possible to develop your skills" (Cummings 1992, 56).

It follows that experts in a particular area are best qualified to recognize creative efforts among their own. The author certainly admits that she would not be able to identify creative efforts in nuclear physics because of her lack of knowledge and understanding of that topic.

Effort

It takes more than a thorough understanding of a topic or skill to be constructively creative in that area. Writers, for example, do not simply sit down, pick up a pen or pull out a computer keyboard, and write great stories; they place a great deal of effort into their writing. This author occasionally talks with authors and illustrators of children's books. When questioned about the motivation, effort, and length of time spent on the book, writer Rudolfo Anaya discussed how he worked hard to produce *The Farolitos of Christmas* (1995). This story is based on the question of how the original Mexican luminaries, built as large fires, were later largely replaced by the small farolitos (lighted candles in sand-filled paper bags). Anaya develops his story around a fictitious, but creative, answer to this question.

Some authors and illustrators claim that great ideas come as "ahas," as in the case of Pat Cummings (1992, 18) who states, "Sometimes, ideas hit me smack in the head when I'm doing something like swimming or reading, or when I'm halfway through a drawing."

Creativity

Definitions of Creativity

Inaccurate labeling of some things as creative at least partially results from the lack of a solid definition for creativity. Some definitions of creativity indicate that it involves novel ideas or products (Piirto 1992; Rogers 1961). Amabile (1989, 15) writes, "A child's behavior is creative if it is novel and appropriate" and E. Paul Torrance (1994, 7) explains creativity as a rational function stating it is

> The process of sensing problems or gaps in informa-
> tion, forming ideas or hypotheses, testing and modify-
> ing this hypothesis, and communicating the results.

This definition is conceivably more informative for those who believe that creativity can be improved through training (Parnes 1988). When instructors train students to be more proficient at discovering and defining problems, we are really inviting creative thinking to develop solutions. It is exciting to visualize the power of a society in which most individuals dedicate themselves to learning about and using creative thinking. This society would be filled with those who were, among other occupations, creative scientists, business people, mathematicians, teachers, and people who work in the arts.

Harman and Rheingold (1984, 14) state that "When we all learn the tricks of the creativity trade that were formerly reserved for geniuses, the masterpiece of our collective endeavors and breakthroughs could be not a painting or a theorem, but a new way of life."

Complexity of Creativity

The act of thinking creatively is a complex process evolving from factors including personality, motivation, circumstance, and divergent and convergent thinking. Many of the chapters in this book describe parts of divergent thinking and provide suggestions for improving skills, such as fluency, flexibility, and originality. Not one of these, alone, represents creative thinking; therefore, teachers are cautioned not to let their efforts become fragmented pieces of the creativity puzzle that result in the development of isolated skills. It is essential that students develop understanding by practicing the individual creative ability and thinking about its connection to creative production. Teachers can emphasize how each creative ability works as a part of the total creative process. For example, fluency is a creative ability that allows students to produce many ideas or solutions; however, these can be meaningless if none of them are original. Elaboration upon an original idea is essential in order for it to be of value. Students who learn and practice creative abilities prepare themselves to analyze their own creative thinking. Analysis of individual creative processes for a given situation yields insight for reproduction of the process in another appropriate situation. Students who identify parts of the process that were difficult can recognize their own specific creative abilities requiring further development. Additionally, students who understand those abilities that aid the creative process are better equipped to function when asked to do an assignment "creatively."

Unfortunately, sometimes creative thinking is more destructive than constructive. Scientists thought creatively when they developed the atomic bomb—something that remains a threat to society. Many criminals use creative thinking toward a destructive end. Even students use creative thinking to get others in trouble or to avoid doing homework.

Facilitating the Development of Creativity

Initial efforts toward creative thinking usually seem somewhat frivolous and simple, such as the following example of brainstorming all of the ways to get to school. Fourth- and fifth-graders might suggest riding a kangaroo, hang gliding over the building and "dropping" in, crawling through a secret tunnel from their houses, or landing in a hot air balloon on the playground. These answers resulted from creative thinking and are unique. While enjoying the fun and humor of activities, such as brainstorming, students become better skilled at thinking creatively and gain confidence in their abilities. This enhances their chances of using productive creative thinking again, when opportunities arise.

Book Format

Teachers often rush to prepare lesson plans and hurriedly glance through activity books to find an exercise pertaining to the topic of the week. While this probably does not cause any problems for students, it does for the teacher. Without prior understanding of the content or process used in the activity, teachers are forced to do exactly what is instructed in the book. Suffice it to say, it is difficult to develop meaningful lessons involving creative thinking without a foundation. This book is designed to alleviate that problem and provide the information and examples needed for teachers to generate their own lessons.

All chapters begin with fundamental information about the chapter topic. In most chapters, this is followed by literature-based activities that may be used as presented or adapted to fit student needs. Each activity falls into sequential segments that may be taught all at once or used individually as shorter lessons. The activities include closure and evaluation procedures, related literature, and ideas for personalizing the lessons. The personalization section includes suggestions for revising lessons to meet the various needs of students. The categories in this section include, Older or More Able Students and Younger or Less Able Students. Please do not restrict any child from an activity that facilitates creative growth! Physically or mentally challenged children need this opportunity as do gifted children. At times, learning disabled or dyslexic children have proven to be more creative than other students. Additionally, their self-image blossoms during successful creative activities.

Many readers may already be well-versed in some of the chapter topics; however, please read through the information at the beginning of the chapters to affirm the knowledge you already possess.

The activities in this book were either written purposely for the author's own students or developed with past students in mind. Experience using them with children has demonstrated the need occasionally to make adaptations, so feel free to add to them or to take out sections and make them right for your students.

Chapter 1
FLUENCY

Nothing is more dangerous than an idea, when it's the only one we have.

Emile Chartier

Definition and Explanation

Fluency is the ability to produce a quantity of ideas, answers, or problem solutions. E. Paul Torrance (1979) discussed fluency as the ability to produce and consider many alternatives. A person who consistently offers multiple ways to complete a project displays fluency, and the student in the classroom who offers many reasons why the teacher should not assign homework is also fluent.

Role of Divergent Questions

Adults encourage children to be fluent by asking divergent questions for which there are no clear-cut answers or limitations to response types. When preparing divergent questions, ask yourself if you know the "correct" answer; if you do, the question is not divergent. Divergent questions encourage students to participate in class without fear of saying the "wrong" thing. For example, this occurs when the teacher asks students a question for which there are many possible answers, such as "how many ways can you use a ruler?" If, however, the teacher asks students a convergent question such as "why do rulers have numbers on them?" the students are led to the "right" answer. Students cannot be fluent when there is only one correct answer. Fluent students will probably be upset when the time for answering a divergent question elapses. Usually, these students are still writing answers, while less fluent students often finish before the allotted time. Table 1.1 compares the responses of a fluent and a less fluent student to the question "How many ways can a ruler be used?"

Table 1.1. Comparison of Student Responses

Responses to "How many ways can a ruler be used?"	
Fluent Student	**Less Fluent Student**
to measure something	for measuring
to draw straight lines	for drawing lines
to make a seesaw for dolls	to hit someone
to bat a ball or something else	
to prop up a window	
to make a hand-held sign	
as a drum major's baton	

Divergent thinking results as students modify an existing product or answer, formulate a new idea, or combine existing ideas in a new way. Divergent thinking differs from convergent thinking for which the idea or question response is derived from existing information. Both types of thinking are important in creativity; however, divergent thinking results in greater fluency.

Fluency is like a barking dog when a burglar comes to your home. The more the dog barks, the better the chances that the burglar will go away. Hopefully, the more ideas generated by fluent thinkers, the better the possibility of finding an exciting idea.

Importance of Fluency

The act of being fluent magnifies the range of possibilities for being creative. It makes statistical sense that when you increase the number of ideas or problem solutions, you also increase the possibilities for producing an applicable solution (Osborn 1963). Teachers who encourage students to consider a range of possibilities free children to think in multiple areas, draw on personal experiences, use multiple intelligences (Gardner 1983), and make new connections. Isn't that what sound educational theory suggests?

Table 1.2 depicts the relationship between sound educational theory and the fluent production of ideas.

Table 1.2. Theory and Fluency Comparison

Educational Theory	Fluent Production of Ideas
• interdisciplinary lessons	• exploration of multiple domains
• lessons tied to personal experience or prior learning	• consideration of ideas previously used and prior experiences
• lessons presented in a variety of forms (visual, auditory, etc.)	• utilization of individual expertise and ways of thinking (multiple intelligences)
• activities that allow students to assimilate and apply new information	• directed consideration of combinations of ideas (making new connections)

Examples of Fluency

Adults

We recognize fluent adults in many domains of work and by a variety of personal characteristics. Musicians quickly produce musical motives or variations on existing melodies which delight audiences. Jazz musicians display this ability when improvising on a basic blues chord progression. Poets and authors use language fluently as do lecturers, politicians, and others.

Children

At times, fluent students continue offering answers to questions after the teacher has tried to move forward with a lesson. These fluent children often irritate teachers, particularly in this educational era of limited lesson time. It is difficult to complete an in-depth lesson before having to take the class to art or physical education, which are also important. Students also display fluency of ideas in nonverbal dimensions, including drawing, interpretation using body movements, and manipulation of objects. A young student displayed this ability when she drew a robot designed to catch a gingerbread man. The students were asked to apply animal characteristics to their robot. While many students drew one or two animal characteristics, such as wings or claws, on their robots, the fluent student applied characteristics from many animals (Meador 1994). This included a rhinoceros horn, duck feet, eagle wings, snail slime, and other features.

Brainstorming

Brainstorming allows students to practice being fluent in a safe environment. This cannot occur without explanation, training, and facilitation, and teachers must present the rules for brainstorming prior to initiation of the activity. Osborn (1963, 156) suggested the following rules:

1. Criticism is ruled out. . . .
2. "Free-wheeling" is welcomed. . . .
3. Quantity is wanted. . . .
4. Combination and improvement are sought. . . .

Teachers need to remind students that they must not judge or comment about any suggestions made by others and that they must not prejudge their own answers. Without such directions, students may not offer an answer that they believe to be "impossible." Younger students do not understand the term "freewheeling," so explain that wild or crazy ideas are encouraged. Also, explain to them how to hitchhike onto other people's ideas by adding new elements. A student who comments "she took my idea" has not learned the hitchhiking rule.

Teachers must enforce the brainstorming rules during the activity and will discover that students have the most difficulty with the first rule. Children are usually good at criticism and find it hard to break a habit; so learning not to criticize is an additional benefit of brainstorming. The first rule helps them to capitalize on an idea and to use the fourth rule. Students learn to take an idea they initially wanted to criticize and to build on some dimension of it to transform it. This is like turning smelly fish into caviar or looking for a pearl in an oyster. Students look for something good in every idea.

Ways to Brainstorm

There are a number of different ways to brainstorm; using variety encourages students to remain interested in the process. Classes could practice brainstorming when transitioning between subjects, waiting to go home or to the lunchroom, or anytime when the group needs a break from what they are doing. Sessions can be either short or long by the teacher simply setting a time limit. For example, in five minutes name possible ways a child could get to school, or brainstorm solutions for saving the rain forests. The amount of time spent depends on how the session goes. Please do not time brainstorming sessions when the result will be used for some purpose. The pressure produced from a ticking clock is not conducive to fluency.

Slip Storms

Late second graders and older elementary students who write reasonably well enjoy slip writing on sticky notes. Rather than brainstorming out loud in a group, students brainstorm independently and write ideas on sticky notes. Students would be expected to use many notes during a brainstorming session. After all the notes are adhered to the board or a chart pad, students arrange the notes into logical categories removing the ideas that are exactly the same and modifying and combining others. This is also a fine example of flexible thinking since the students note they have chosen ideas from a variety of angles.

Individual Storms

Students prepare individual lists of items, ideas, or problem solutions during the allotted time in class or at home. Later, they combine the lists easily when one student reads his or her list out loud and the other students cross duplications off their own lists. Each student has an opportunity to read until there are no other new answers.

Technology Storms

Some computer systems in schools are linked so that students at different monitors can share typed information. Several students can create individually brainstormed lists, send them to one another electronically, and combine them on screen for printing.

Hitchhiking Storms

Small groups of students receive short lists of possible answers to a brainstorming question. Each group attempts to piggyback on the answers and tries to create as many new ideas as possible. Here is an example concerning how students can share information after school hours.

List Provided by Adult

1. Write a letter.
2. Call the person on the phone.
3. Go over to the person's house and share information.
4. Ask someone else to tell the person.

Children's Hitchhiking List

1. Send an E-mail.
2. Fax the person the information.
3. Yell really loud at the person.
4. Meet the person somewhere in between your homes.
5. Put a note on the person's dog and send it home to the person.

SCAMPER

SCAMPER is not a brainstorming method; however, many use it to help generate ideas. Bob Eberle (1971) developed the acronym *SCAMPER* for a self-questioning technique originated by Alex Osborn (1963). Each letter represents a key word that stimulates the production of ideas. It is suggested that students think about some of these words when they are having trouble brainstorming or to locate that one outstanding idea.

SCAMPER represents the following words:

S - substitute

C - combine

A - adapt

M - modify, magnify, minify

P - put to other uses

E - eliminate

R - reverse, rearrange

In the lesson presented later in this chapter, which is based upon *The Tree That Would Not Die* (Levine 1995), students brainstorm solutions regarding how to help a poisoned tree. Using *SCAMPER*, during a lull in production of ideas, the teacher could ask the students to envision the tree as small as a book (**Mi**nimize) and think of how they could help a tree that size. Ideas generated from minimization may suggest plausible solutions for a regular-sized tree.

In another lesson, students brainstorming a list of what they would like to do with the character in *Miss Tizzy* (Gray 1993) could be asked to **Eliminate** the fact that Miss Tizzy always remained in and around her house when she played with neighborhood children. Students may think about where they could play with Miss Tizzy outside the neighborhood.

SCAMPER also serves as a wonderful aid when teachers design questions to elicit creative thinking outside a brainstorming session. The following questions, based on *SCAMPER*, may be used after reading one of the many versions of the story, "Little Red Riding Hood." These questions were previously published in a full article about *SCAMPER* (Meador 1996).

- **Combine:** What would happen if your pet bear went to Grandmother's house with you?
- **Put to Other Uses:** How else could Red Riding Hood use her basket when she got to Grandmother's house?
- **Minify:** What could the wolf do to make his eyes look smaller?
- **Substitute:** Think of yourself as Red Riding Hood. What would you do to the wolf if you had hot chili powder in your basket instead of cookies?
- **Rearrange:** How would the story end if Grandmother went to visit Red Riding Hood and the wolf were in Red's house?

Summary

Teachers and students who practice and learn to value fluency prepare themselves for other necessary components of the creative process. Many of the most highly original and productive ideas surface at the end of a brainstorming episode, after the group feels it has exhausted all other possibilities. Practice in brainstorming encourages students to generate multiple ideas before deciding to use just one. Using brainstorming rules also helps students learn to value their own ideas.

PROBLEM SOLVING WITH *MISS TIZZY*

Content: **Social Studies and Literature**

Creativity: **Fluency**

Book Selection: Miss Tizzy **by Libba Moore Gray (1993)**

> **Concepts in Book Selection**
>
> People of different races and ages can be friends.
>
> Friends care about each other and help one another.
>
> Older people are capable of doing things.

The character, Miss Tizzy, demonstrates fluency as she thinks of many ways to entertain the neighborhood children. They bake cookies, make puppets, have a parade, and do many other things. When Miss Tizzy becomes ill and can no longer play with them, these children display problem-solving skills. They eventually entertain Miss Tizzy outside her bedroom window using what they learned from her.

The book depicts the human cycle: The old woman teaches the young, and they reciprocate her kindness when she is ill. Even though the illustrations of the character Miss Tizzy depict her as fragile at the end of the book, she remains colorful and full of life. This book portrays the fact that the elderly have much to share with others and demonstrates that it is not necessary to hold a paying job in order to contribute to society.

Lesson Capsule

Students brainstorm things they would like to do in their own neighborhood. They listen to the story, *Miss Tizzy*. Finally, the students use their brainstorming list to create their own product.

Lesson Objectives

The students will

♦ practice fluency by generating a list during brainstorming,

♦ observe book characters' skills of fluency and problem solving,

♦ identify acts of kindness and the importance of companionship, and

♦ personalize the story by creating an original product.

Procedures

1. Briefly discuss things the children do at home to have fun. Help them realize that some activities require adult supervision. Ask students to brainstorm a list of things they could do in their own neighborhood with three or four other children and an adult. Ask them to

exclud e anything that requires vehicular transportation. Remind students about the rules of brainstorming.

2. List all ideas—even the crazy ones—on a chart pad or blackboard.

Intermediate Closure and Evaluation. Discuss brainstorming and the fact that many answers were possible—not just one. Explain to the students that they were fluent. Ask them what they learned from this lesson and how they feel about the process. Evaluate the objective, "The students will practice fluency," by observing whether all students participate in the brainstorming activity.

3. Discuss the cover picture of the book, *Miss Tizzy*. Students may notice relative ages of the characters as well as their ethnicities. Miss Tizzy is black, and the children appear to be of various races. Ask students to look at the cover and to guess what the older woman is doing with the children. How would the students expect the woman to spend her time with them? What might they do together?

4. Read the book.

5. Question students about the story. Include some of the following:
   a. What were some of the many different activities the children and Miss Tizzy enjoyed?
   b. Do you think Miss Tizzy was fluent?
   c. What did the neighborhood adults think about Miss Tizzy's activities?
   d. Did the children feel the same way? Why or why not?
   e. How did Miss Tizzy know what the children would enjoy?
   f. Why did Miss Tizzy have time to play with the children when most of the other adults did not? (Discuss companionship.)
   g. If you were a child in Miss Tizzy's neighborhood, how would you feel when she got sick?
   h. What sort of problem did the children experience when Miss Tizzy became ill? How did they solve the problem?

Intermediate Closure and Evaluation. Discuss why problem solving was important to the children in *Miss Tizzy*. Do students think these children brainstormed many ideas before deciding what to do? How could brainstorming be used in the classroom? Advise students to watch for times when being fluent would be helpful.

Optional Extended Closure: Borrow a "dress-up box" or some unusual hats for students to wear, and lead a class parade, similar to the one in the book, around the school parking lot.

6. Tell the students that some day, a person like Miss Tizzy might come to the students' neighborhood. Use their brainstorming list to discuss things they could do together.

7. Allow students to choose their projects. The following choices are appropriate:
   a. Rewrite the story about Miss Tizzy using your own neighborhood and creating activities from the class list. (Students might write about a single day's events.)
   b. Act out the book using appropriate props or costumes, if needed.
   c. Organize activities that you could do with people at a senior citizens' center.
   d. Write a letter to a grandparent or other relative discussing activities you have planned for their next visit.

Closure and Final Evaluation

8. The type of closure depends upon the project chosen in the preceding section; however, closure should include a time to share ideas after the project's completion. Ask how the projects show that there are many "right" answers. Observe students while they work on the projects. Do they generate many ideas before solving their project-planning problems?

Personalizing the Lesson

Older or More Able Students

Students can use this lesson for delving into a topic of their own interest. Miss Tizzy planned activities for the neighborhood children based on her realm of experiences and knowledge of what children like to do. Altering Miss Tizzy's character and background would change the activities she develops. For example, a student interested in archaeology could describe Miss Tizzy as an important person in that field. This Miss Tizzy would arrange for her neighborhood children to go out for a dig in a field or to visit a museum, or she might present a slide show of her archaeological expeditions. The following is a list of possible former occupations for Miss Tizzy:

- mapmaker
- swimming instructor
- scientist
- zookeeper
- doctor
- aerobics teacher
- librarian
- mountain climber
- inventor

Younger or Less Able Students

Some students may need to work with the teacher in small rotating groups and be guided through the product phase of the lesson. This segment is difficult when students are unable to read the brainstorming list. These students may wish to cut pictures from catalogs that depict what activities they would like to do with Miss Tizzy. The toy section of most department store catalogs provides ample ideas. The story could be told by having each child describe a single day with Miss Tizzy.

Related Literature

Miss Tizzy and other carefully chosen stories deal with the delicate subject of aging. Books about older people should largely depict them as valuable and enjoyable companions. Teachers seeking other stories that describe this segment of the life cycle will enjoy *The Gift of Driscoll Lipscomb* by Sara Yamaka (1995), described in the originality chapter, and *The Wind Garden* by Angela McAllister and Claire Fletcher (1994) found in the flexibility chapter.

Also, *Song and Dance Man* by Karen Ackerman (1988), which won the 1989 Caldecott Award, tells the story of a grandfather whose grandchildren enjoy being with him. They like to watch him sing and dance and value their grandfather for his special abilities without concern for his age.

The grandmother in *The Patchwork Quilt* by Valerie Flournoy (1985) uses fabric scraps from various family members to make her masterpiece quilt. Her granddaughter and the rest of the family work on the quilt while she is ill, until she can resume her work.

SAVING THE TREES: A LESSON IN HUMANITY

Content: **Social Studies and Science**

Creativity: **Fluency**

Book Selection: The Tree That Would Not Die **by Ellen Levine (1995)**

Concepts in Book Selection

Every living thing has a life cycle.

People who work together are productive.

Some people commit crimes against nature.

The Tree That Would Not Die by Ellen Levine (1995) reveals the true story of the Treaty Oak in Austin, Texas. Levine and illustrator Ted Rand lead readers through the growth of the oak, from a small sapling in the woods 500 years ago to the present. The tree tells the story and includes its opinions about what it saw over its lifetime, and its abstract and physical feelings. The tree, which is located in Austin, Texas, describes the rich history of this area, from an era when buffalo roamed in the wild, through wars, to the present day. The author contrasts the tree's heritage, during which people left it standing, against the pain the tree feels when someone tried to destroy it. The book ends with the true story of how people joined together to save the Treaty Oak.

Fluency of ideas is reflected in the book when its characters think of many different solutions for saving the tree. A variety of individuals, from scientists to school children, address the problem.

The tree acts as a great-great-grandfather, who has seen a long span of history and tells it from a unique perspective, which adds personal value to the historical information. This book is also marvelous for teaching about cooperation and showing how many different people can work together for the benefit of something they care about.

Someday a Tree by Eve Bunting (1993) tells a similar story, but without historical information. It is a shorter, simpler book about a girl, her parents, and others, who try to save a tree that is dying as a result of pollution. *Someday a Tree* may be substituted in this lesson and would be more appropriate for very young children.

Lesson Capsule

The lesson spans a minimum of one week. The students listen to and discuss the book, *The Tree That Would Not Die.* Finally, they brainstorm ways to protect trees from modern problems. Products suggested in this lesson evolve from creative movement, action, and song writing.

Lesson Objectives

The students will

♦ gain empathy for living things,

♦ understand the length of a large tree's life,

♦ practice fluency by seeking solutions to a problem, and

♦ understand the power of people working together toward a common goal.

Procedures

Optional: Allow the students to create a wall-sized oak tree with a broad trunk. If you do not have enough brown paper, grocery bags may be used. Show the children how to create individual leaves. When the students are out of the room, detach leaves, allowing them to fall on the floor. Detach just a few each day to create the effect that the tree is dying. Question the students regarding why a tree might die.

1. Read *The Tree That Would Not Die* by Ellen Levine.

2. The following questions and discussion items are appropriate.

    • Why would anyone want to kill a tree? (List answers on chart paper.)

    • Is it ever necessary and appropriate to kill a tree? When?

    • Discuss the many things that the tree witnessed throughout history. How much time did the tree's history span?

    • What other living things are as old as the tree?

    • How did the man in the story try to kill the Treaty Oak?

    • What else could happen to a large tree to cause its destruction? (Encourage the students to think about both natural and human causes.)

    • *Optional:* Discuss the brief history of the tree the students made.

    • How did people work together to try to save the Treaty Oak?

    • If the tree in their room were real and it were dying, what types of things could the class do to save it? Would it help to work as a group?

Intermediate Evaluation and Closure. Check for understanding of the last three objectives during the discussion of the book: Discussion following the questions helps to evaluate whether students understand the length of a large tree's life; answers to other questions indicate students' understanding of the power of people working together toward a common goal; and brainstorming ways to protect a real tree in their classroom assists students in practicing fluency.

3. Students work individually or in small groups to create their own project depicting the tree as it starts to die. Suggestions include expression through creative movement, poetry, original songs, or art work.

    Students enjoy working with soft music playing in the background. It seems to make them more free to express themselves. Piano samplers on the Windham Hill Music label are often suitable.

4. Students and teachers are often less comfortable with products involving creative movement or singing. The following suggestions may prove helpful.

Creative Movement or Actions

Younger students have less difficulty than older students with creative movement. Late second- or third-graders may need to begin in a structured manner by interpreting *The Giving Tree* by Shel Silverstein (1964). Someone reads the story out loud while small groups of students create the effect of parts of the tree gently falling away until there is only one small person left representing the tree stump. It is appropriate to position students at various heights, with some standing on chairs or stools. Practice with this or other similar stories prepares students to create their own interpretation of *The Tree That Would Not Die*.

Original Songs

Begin by asking students to change the words to a common tune, such as "Mary Had a Little Lamb." Words appropriate for *The Tree That Would Not Die* follow:

Verse 1. Texas had a little tree, little tree, little tree
Texas had a little tree, which grew up big and strong.
Verse 2. And it lived through history, history, history
And it lived through history, until one awful day . . .

Small groups (2 to 3 students) work well when composing lyrics. More musically advanced students who want to write their own melody may enjoy "doodling" with various tonal ideas. It is fun for them to use telephone numbers to create a melody. Students first number the tones of any scale. They sing or play these tones in the order of their telephone numbers. For a reasonably sad sounding song, students will have good luck starting on the note D and using no flats or sharps (dorian mode). An example follows:

Dorian	D E F G A B C D E F	Phone Number: 351-7751
Mode	1 2 3 4 5 6 7 8 9 0	Melody: F A D C C A D

Students begin with this musical idea, then may alter any tones that they dislike to develop a song. Children then use any instrument or voice to work on the melody. Some students may use a small electronic keyboard or violin, while others may use musical computer programs. A set of handbells works well, or scale tones may be created by tapping on glasses filled with varying levels of water. Nonmusicians easily participate when the keys, handbells, or glasses have been numbered according to scale tones. The haunting sound that often results can be used as part of the creative dramatization of the tree's plight.

Closure and Evaluation

Students perform group or individual products. Teachers watch for signs of empathy for living things displayed by students in their work. In conclusion, students should express what they learned from their project and how they were fluent.

Personalizing the Lesson

Older or More Able Students

These students will be challenged if they have opportunities to generate information or to share existing information in a unique form. Several different suggestions follow.

1. Choose another type of tree and place it in another state, such as a cedar tree in Washington. Give students a range of years during which the tree lived. Have them investigate the history and suggest events that might have occurred near this tree.

2. Have students draw a mural illustrating the Treaty Oak, surrounded by other trees, animals, or buildings. They animate the drawing by adding speech balloons. These various objects or living things in the mural discuss the history of the area or look for solutions when the tree is poisoned.

Younger or Less Able Students

These students may enjoy creating "save the tree" posters.

Related Literature

The Fall of Freddie the Leaf by Leo Buscaglia (1982)
   Buscaglia provides readers with a lovely description of the life cycle of leaves in *The Fall of Freddie the Leaf*. Conversations between leaves on a tree provide opportunities for readers to gain empathy for them. This book is a marvelous contrast to *The Tree That Would Not Die*, because the leaf, Freddie, declines through natural causes and the Treaty Oak's problems resulted from human deviance.

Tree Man by Carmen Agra Deedy (1993)
   Teachers who wish to integrate a light-hearted book about trees into the lesson appreciate Carmen Deedy's humorous book, *Tree Man*. This story, set in a South American rain forest, involves a boa named Ana Conda, a sloth called Slow Jim, and an odd toucan named Bill. They are, of course, "tree amigos." Their Christmastime confusion over a gift from the North Pole is at the heart of the story. The tree amigos give up their most prized possessions in order to have gifts to give the Tree Man, who is from the North Pole.

Fishermen use fluent and flexible thinking when preparing their tackle box. They must think of many types of bait to take along on their fishing trip.

Additional Activity for Developing Fluency

Rhyme Storms

Teachers of young children usually have a very thick file of nursery rhyme activities; yet, other, more purposeful activities are usually welcomed. Isaksen, Dorval, and Treffinger (1996) discuss a classroom episode in which a first grade teacher asked her students to brainstorm, or rhyme storm, ways to help Humpty Dumpty avoid falling to his demise. Many nursery rhymes present characters who have problems or are doing something questionable. These are appropriate for use in developing fluency. Consider the following questions based on nursery rhymes:

Why was Little Jack Horner sitting in a corner?

What might Mary do to keep her little lamb from following her to school?

Another type of rhyme storm is appropriate for the development or assessment of content.

Procedure

1. Students generate possibilities for substitutions in typical nursery rhymes. For instance, they might brainstorm a list of other insects that could sit down beside Miss Muffet.

   Original Rhyme
   Little Miss Muffet
   Sat on a tuffet,
   Eating her curds and whey;
   There came a big spider,
   Who sat down beside her
   And frightened Miss Muffet away.

   This rhyme storm is appropriate for assessment of content knowledge following lessons on insects. While students generate ideas, the teacher determines which students, if any, need further opportunities to work on the content.

   Brainstormed List

ants	termites	mosquitoes
beetles	flies	gnats
wasps	crickets	aphids
bees	butterflies	grubs

2. Students choose one insect from the brainstormed list and substitute it for the word "spider" in the original rhyme.
   Optional: Younger students need to generate several rhyming words for the new insect before proceeding to step 3. Students who choose a fly might generate rhyming words such as try, my, cry, dry, why, and so forth.

3. Students then change the rest of "Little Miss Muffet" to rhyme with the new word.

> **Revised**
> Little Miss Muffet
> Sat on a tuffet,
> Eating her curds and whey;
> There came a big fly,
> Who sat down to cry
> And caused her to scurry away.

> **Revised**
> Little Miss Muffet
> Sat on a tuffet,
> Eating her curds and whey;
> There came some small ants,
> Who sat on her pants
> And frightened Miss Muffet away.

Closure

It is fun for students to dramatize their new nursery rhymes. Allow them to elaborate upon the rhyme's character and actions by supplying dress-up clothes that students don for their performances. Just adding a hat to the drama can elicit more theatrical interpretations.

Included below are two other examples of rhyme storms:

> **Original Rhyme**
> Little Jack Horner
> Sat in a corner,
> Eating a Christmas pie
> He stuck in his thumb
> And pulled out a plum,
> And said "What a good boy am I!"

What else could Jack have been eating or drinking while he was in the corner?

cola	chocolate cake
juice	popcorn
Hawaiian Punch	jelly beans
cookies	

> **Revised**
> Little Jack Horner
> Sat in a corner
> Drinking Hawaiian Punch
> He filled a big mug
> And spilled on the rug,
> And said "I messed up a bunch!"

Additional Nursery Rhymes for Rhyme Storms

> Peter, Peter, pumpkin eater,
> Had a wife and couldn't keep her.
> He put her in a pumpkin shell
> And there he kept her, very well.

- What else could Peter eat?
- Exchange Peter's name with another that begins with a different letter, such as "d": Donald, Donald, Donut Eater.

> Little drops of water
> Little grains of sand
> Make a mighty ocean
> And the pleasant land.

- Think of how other things are formed, such as a house made of sturdy boards of wood, and nails, that are so strong; or clothes, made from bolts of pretty fabric and stitches carefully sewn.

> Daffy-Down-Dilly
> Has come to town
> In a yellow petticoat
> And a green gown.

- Use another letter, such as "s," to build the name, Suzy-Sarah-Simple, in this rhyme.

Younger children who are learning about colors may substitute their own colored pictures of a petticoat and a gown for the words in the last line of the rhyme.

> There was an old woman who lived in a shoe.
> She had so many children, she didn't know what to do.
> She gave them some broth,
> Without any bread,
> She whipped them all soundly, and put them to bed.

- Where else could the woman live?
- What would contemporary children eat?

Additional Books in Which Characters Are Fluent

Too Many Pumpkins by Linda White (1996)

Rebecca Estelle, who lives with her cat, Esmeralda, hates pumpkins. Once, when she was young and money was scarce, she had to eat pumpkins for breakfast, lunch, and dinner. Now she never wants to see one again, so she takes special care to keep the pumpkins out of her garden. One day, however, a pumpkin falls off a truck and into her yard. Its seeds grow, even as Rebecca Estelle ignores them. By fall, so many pumpkins have grown that Rebecca Estelle makes them into sweets, and the whole town comes to visit her and enjoy them. She and Esmeralda have such a wonderful time that she keeps seeds for planting the next year.

Rebecca Estelle demonstrates fluency by baking many different kinds of food with the pumpkins. Students may enjoy talking about concocting dishes made with chocolate instead of pumpkin. They can peruse cookbooks to get ideas.

Short Activity

Teresa Gilbreath, a teacher in Georgia, suggests using orange paper jack-o'-lantern cutouts to give students an opportunity to use original thinking. Students cut their jack-o'-lanterns in half down the line of symmetry and separate them into two parts. Students then brainstorm what the new pieces resemble. Next, they draw a picture on which they glue the jack-o'-lantern halves to represent part of the illustration. Students may use the jack-o'-lantern halves as ears for creatures, turtles crawling on the ground, butterfly nets, and other clever things. This activity obviously ties into math concepts and encourages flexible thinking.

Miss Nelson Is Missing! by Harry Allard and James Marshall (1977)

Miss Nelson, a teacher with a sweet voice, has the worst class in the whole school. The students are rude and refuse to do their work. Miss Nelson knows that she must do something. One day, Miss Nelson does not come to school, but a strange women named Miss Viola Swamp appears in an ugly black dress to teach the class. Miss Swamp puts the children to work and does not allow them to have story time or any other freedom. She assigns a great deal of homework and generally makes the students' lives miserable. They long for Miss Nelson to return and demonstrate fluency and flexibility as they think of many things that may have happened to her. These include thoughts that have Miss Nelson going to Mars or being taken by a swarm of butterflies. Finally, Miss Nelson returns to the classroom, and the students are so relieved that they decide to behave. Miss Nelson is also relieved that she will not need her ugly black dress again this year.

Students can list other things that might have happened to Miss Nelson when she was away from the classroom. Gather students into groups of four or five, and have each group start a list of ideas. Rather than brainstorming as a small group, students can pass the list to one another and have each person add a new idea. This is a quiet group project.

King Bidgood's in the Bathtub by Audrey Wood (1985)

There is a problem in the kingdom: King Bidgood will not get out of the bathtub to carry out his duties. The Page alerts the other court members, each of whom thinks they have the solution to the problem. Fluency is demonstrated in this story as court members think of a variety of ways to get the King out of the tub. These include enticing the King to go fishing, eat lunch, or fight a battle. Finally, the Page gets to the bottom of the problem, by pulling the plug on the tub so that the water disappears, forcing the King to get out of the tub.

The humorous pictures in this book, created by Don Wood, motivate students to think of many other ways to encourage the King to get out of the bathtub. Students may brainstorm ideas and then create a series of pictures depicting the solutions.

The Wing Shop by Elvira Woodruff (1991)

When Matthew moves to a different house across town, he misses his old neighborhood and his friends. He wants to go back for a visit, but he cannot drive, take the bus, or travel on foot that far alone. Then Matthew discovers a special store, the Wing Shop, where people can rent wings by the hour. The pictures in this story and the many types of wings Matthew tries depict fluency resulting from the author's consideration of all sorts of winged things. Silly things happen to Matthew when he dons different wings, but he finally does fly over his old neighborhood. Ultimately, he decides to stay in his new house.

Short Activity

Young children especially enjoy dramatizing this story by demonstrating how they would fly wearing various types of wings. They also enjoy making wings for small toy creatures. A clever teacher can turn this into a science activity by allowing students to experiment with various sizes, weights, types, and materials on the wings. Which ones work the best and why? Does the addition of a breeze from an electric fan change anything?

The Boy Who Had Wings by Jane Yolen (1974)

Consider this book as a sophisticated follow-up to *The Wing Shop*, or use it with older readers. It is a serious story about a boy who was born with wings and tried to hide them until a near tragedy caused him to fly freely. This is a sensitive story about caring and learning to be who you are. The characters in this book do not model fluency; however, students could consider numerous ways in which the boy's family and others might have helped him.

When I'm Sleepy by Jane R. Howard (1985)

This simple book tells and illustrates many different places a sleepy little girl might rest. These include curling up in a basket, crawling into a cave, and sleeping on a log. In each of the beautiful, peaceful drawings, the child is pictured asleep with animals. Fluency of ideas is obvious due to the number of places she thinks about sleeping.

Things to Brainstorm: Spur-of-the-Moment Ideas

General

- How many ways can you use a yardstick?
- Name many reasons why there is a hole in the center of a donut.
- List excuses for leaving your homework at home.

Language Arts

- Names things in the kitchen that begin with the letter C.
- Create as many three-letter words as possible that end in "op." If you invent a word, create a definition for it.

- Name action verbs that could be in a story about a superhero.
- List as many adjectives as possible for the person in this picture. (Provide picture of individual—this works best if a background environment is shown.)

Math—Science

- Where does a plastic cup go when it is thrown in the river?
- Name different things you could use to measure your desk.
- Name different ways to measure the amount of water in a container.

Social Studies

- Name different ways you could get to school.
- What names that begin with the letter A could be given to children? (Invented names are okay if the children can pronounce them.)
- Create a list of places to go on a summer vacation.
- Look at the map of the community. Show various routes from the school to the grocery store. (Any route is allowed.)

Chapter 2
FLEXIBILITY

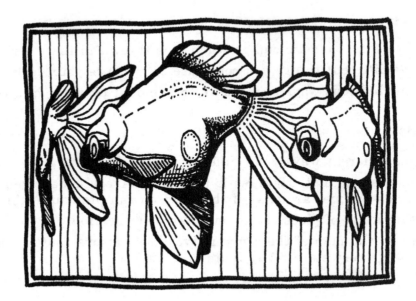

Flexibility is like a cat who hunts for mice in a variety of locations. The cat increases the likelihood of finding a good dinner by being willing to move on and search other places, rather than waiting by a single mouse hole. Flexible thinking increases the probability of success because it encourages the selection of ideas from many different categories or perspectives.

Definition and Explanation

Flexibility is "the ability to take different approaches to a problem, think of ideas in different categories, or view a situation from several perspectives" (Davis and Rimm 1994, 189).

20

Importance of Flexibility

Flexible thinking is valuable in creativity because it moves thought patterns out of natural ruts. If a person drives home from work the same way each day, he or she constantly views the same scenery; however, if the person takes a different route, there are new things to view. Similarly, flexibility in thinking helps create new views.

Examples of Flexibility

Many people, for example, have a difficult time choosing something different to give a family member for a birthday. Perhaps a child always gets the typical type of art materials such as:

crayons	colored pencils
markers	colored chalk
paints	

All of these objects fall into the category of things to use in art; therefore, the person making the list did not demonstrate flexibility. To make a change, consider the following list of ideas for a child's small gift that are products of flexible thinking and include various categories:

paint	crayons
brightly colored ball	picture book
coin purse	

The second list illustrates flexible thinking since the items come from categories including art supplies, reading materials, play objects, and useful things.

Teachers ask children to use flexibility when trying to solve arguments, such as who was first to be playing with a ball, whose turn is it to hand out papers, or who should be the line leader. When teachers ask students to examine the situation from the other child's perspective, they expect the students to be flexible. This is difficult for children while in the "heat of battle"; therefore, adults should provide opportunities for children to practice taking the other person's perspective and using flexible thinking during less threatening situations.

"Who," "what," "when," and "where" questions stimulate flexible thinking by suggesting individuals consider specific sides of an issue. The questions that follow are adaptable for many situations; however, they may make more sense if based on a specific issue. Consider students trying to decide how to organize their classroom so that those who require isolation for studying will have what they need. Students would be reminded to look at the situation from new perspectives or viewpoints before the teacher poses these questions.

Who: Does anyone need to make a particular change in order for a solution to work? Is there someone from outside the class who could help solve the problem?

What: Think about the physical materials that could be used to solve the problem. What must the solution do? Do individuals need silence, visual isolation, or something else? What are the ways in which each of these could be achieved?

When: Is there a particular time when everyone needs isolation? Is there a time when only a few people need isolation? Is it possible to change the time of certain activities to alleviate the problem?

Where: Are there rules that confine the solution to a particular location? In other words, could the problem be solved outside the classroom? If rules exist, how could they be stretched to solve the problem? Can any restrictions be changed?

People tend to rely on their past experiences with a problem when seeking a solution, and at times this is quite limiting. For example, during work on specific school problems, committees often dwell on what they previously did, while those new to the school rely on what was done at their former school. While this is occasionally highly productive, it is plausible that better solutions may be derived by thinking about the issue from other angles. If people imagine the problem without any constraining factors, they often produce important ideas that can be modified and used. Money often appears to be a common barrier to solutions: yet some solvers occasionally ponder pie-in-the-sky solutions, pretending to have all the funding they need. If a brilliant idea occurs, ways to eliminate this constraint often surface.

Flexibility enables artists to visualize forms from a variety of angles, while searching for a kernel of an idea upon which to build. For example, if an artist saw only a face when looking at a circle, it would be difficult to think of other things the form might become; yet, opening the mind to other possibilities may result in a more interesting drawing. A circle could also be the end of a tunnel, a peephole with an eye looking through it, or the inside of an ear.

Classroom Activities

Students who exercise flexible thinking often have ideas that originate from many different subject areas and from both real and imaginary experiences. This is one of the reasons the answers that creative thinkers offer to some questions seem so "off the wall." These students have the marvelous ability to think flexibly and look at things from a variety of perspectives.

Brainstorming provides opportunities for flexibility, and teachers can encourage students to be flexible through questioning during the activity. When students appear to be stymied, ask them to think in different categories. For example, when brainstorming the ways to rearrange the classroom, students will typically suggest ways to move furniture within the floor space of the room. Asking specific, categorical questions, one at a time, may help them generate other ideas. The following questions are based on a technique known as *SCAMPER* developed by Bob Eberle (1990), further explained in Chapter 1. Each letter of this acronym represents an action word.

SCAMPER

Eliminate: Can anything be eliminated or changed in some way?

Modify: Does everything have to remain on the floor?

Ideas produced by flexible thinking in this example involving elimination or modification might include moving the classroom's small couch into the hall for everyone to use, placing a bookcase on top of a table, or hanging the in-basket from the ceiling.

Flexible thinking includes the ability to generate alternative means for presenting information. Teachers model this when they use puppets to give instructions, videotape themselves demonstrating a process, or tape-record information for students. Try to use a variety of formats when presenting a report or other information, and encourage students to follow your model. Book reports do not always need to be written; students can put their ideas to a familiar tune to describe a character or tape-record a fictitious interview with the author or a book character.

Many opportunities for flexibility arise when students work on critical thinking skills. These include identifying fact and opinion, bias and stereotype, and relevant and irrelevant information, among other things. When students analyze and evaluate, they flexibly consider angles, possibilities, and consequences.

The use of integrated curricula and interdisciplinary studies (Charbonneau and Reider 1995; Jacobs 1989; Stepien, Gallagher, and Workman 1993) stimulates students to use flexible thinking by helping them make new connections. Theme development, a popular approach to writing classroom curricula, emphasizes the use of information and skills from a variety of disciplines to build the concept on which the theme is based. For instance, instructors in the 1990 Creative Scholars Program explored the concept of flight during their summer program. They learned to analyze the term from a variety of perspectives as they discussed and worked with ideas about human flight from countries in turmoil, the flight of various types of aircraft and winged animals, and flight of the human spirit and thought.

Flexibility is like going fishing in deep water with a big net. If fishermen throw out their nets and catch only one kind of fish, they realize that they must move their boats to a new location in order to catch different kinds of fish. Remember to help children move their boats!

Summary

Flexibility is highly necessary for creative thinking and for life. Students who learn to be flexible thinkers are better prepared to adapt to changes, ranging from going somewhere else to eat dinner when the pizza restaurant is closed to handling the changes that occur when parents divorce. Flexible children make life interesting by thinking of things to do when bored and of new ways to handle assignments, and by offering new perspectives during discussions.

SEEING THE LIGHT

Content: **Social Studies—Cultural Traditions**
   Language Arts—Languages and Dialects
Creativity: **Flexibility**
*Book Selection: **The Farolitos of Christmas** by Rudolfo Anaya (1995)*

Concepts in Book Selection

Cultures have important traditions.

Children can help solve problems.

Sometimes, family members have to be gone from home.

In some places, it is customary at Christmas to light bright luminaries, sand-filled paper bags with candles inside. The pastores (shepherds) traditionally stopped by the luminaries and sang before going to the church on Christmas Eve. Originally, the luminaries were fires built from small stacks of pinion logs. This story describes a family for which there is no one to chop the pinion logs and chronicles their efforts to find another way to make the luminaries. A young girl, Luz, uses flexible thinking when trying to find other ways to make an outdoor light. Initially, she thinks the family can put candles outside; however, Luz quickly realizes they will blow out in the wind. She also discusses putting the candles in cans so they will not blow out, but concludes that light could not be seen through the cans. Finally, while purchasing a bag of sugar at the store, Luz realizes that light can be seen through paper bags. The family creates beautiful luminaries by placing sand in the bottom of small paper bags and adding candles.

Luz exemplifies characteristics of a flexible thinker by remaining open to possibilities without becoming discouraged. A flexible thinker attacks problems from many different angles. Luz also demonstrates an "aha" experience at the store where she purchases sugar when she has a flash of enlightenment that leads to the solution.

Lesson Capsule

After listening to the story, students discuss that the purpose of the luminaries in the story is to attract the pastores, who will sing before going to church. They list multiple reasons why people might stop by a home at various times of the year. Students exercise flexible thinking by creating substitutions for the luminaries that would attract the pastores to a home.

Lesson Objectives

The students will

◆ practice flexibility while generating ideas,

◆ observe how the book character exercised flexibility in order to solve a problem, and

◆ originate alternative methods for fulfilling the purpose of the luminaries.

Procedures

1. Prepare students for *The Farolitos of Christmas* by finding San Juan in northern New Mexico on the map. If possible, find someone who speaks Spanish to tape-record a greeting to the students. Tape recordings of Hispanic music add another dimension that helps students connect with the culture. Allow students to look at the pictures in the book to gain an understanding of the environment and people depicted in this story.

2. Help the children learn the Spanish vocabulary used in this story. Let them enjoy sharing sentences that use some of the words. They should get used to hearing them before listening to the story. For example, students might try the following:

   My abuelo is very old.
   I wish I had a farolito.
   I like the cookie you brought to me. Gracias.
   I have never seen pastores.

3. Tape-record the words in this book and allow students to hear it at a listening center, or read the words aloud. Students may want to hear the story more than once before embarking on activities pertaining to the book. Do not rush this step.

4. Partner the students and ask them to find out why the characters in the story always build luminaries on Christmas Eve. Lead students to the understanding that the luminaries encourage the shepherds to stop and sing before going to church.

5. Ask small groups to make a list of people they would like to have stop by their houses. The list might include grandparents, school friends, a cartoon character, or a famous football player. Try to get students to limit the list to four or five people.

6. Have students share their lists and discuss how their answers represent flexible thinking because their answers fall under several different categories.

7. Each small group of students should choose two of the people on their original list. Tell students it is their job to ensure that these people come to their houses for a special evening. For example, how would students entice a football player to come to their house? How would they entice their friends to come over on another night? (Beware: students quickly realize that if they can get someone famous to come to their house, other people will also visit. Be sure they understand the guests are invited on different nights.) Students should use flexible thinking and brainstorm the different ways to entice people they have chosen. Guide students toward an understanding that different people have special reasons for visiting.

8. Students in each group simulate their answers by dramatizing their solution.

Closure

Individual students briefly write why they would like a friend to come to their house. They should include their appropriate actions for arranging for the friend to visit.

Evaluation

Ask each group of students to explain how they used flexibility during their work. Observe and note individual use of flexibility during brainstorming and solution-finding. Be sure to watch for inflexibility and design further lessons to help these students think in multiple categories or from varied viewpoints.

Optional Extension

Books such as *The Farolitos of Christmas* make students aware of the differences in cultures and provide a basis for teachers to indicate that these differences should be prized. Wise teachers also discuss similarities between cultures, while being careful not to indicate that we should all do the same things. This is achieved by pointing out not only similarities in actions, such as going to school or playing outdoors, but also similarities in hopes and dreams. *My Wish for Tomorrow*, prepared by the United Nations (1995), presents the wishes of children from many different countries. Students notice that children from different places share common desires. It is appropriate to ask students to think seriously about their wishes for tomorrow, in terms of themselves, others, and the world, prior to sharing children's thoughts from other cultures.

Personalizing the Lesson

Older or More Able Students

Research other cultures to determine if they have any traditions similar to the luminaries.

For example, many people turn on their porch lights for Halloween so that children will know to come to their house for treats. Ask them to think flexibly about alternatives to these traditions, but please remind students that their new ideas may not be acceptable in the culture unless it was absolutely necessary to make a change. It is vital for cultures to preserve their traditions as much as possible.

Younger or Less Able Students

1. Encourage these students to continue exploring substitutions for the luminaries. They may design and draw something other than the farolitos to produce light for the shepherds.

2. When appropriate and safe, allow students to build their solutions.

Related Literature

Chato's Kitchen by Gary Soto (1996)

Soto's work, which falls into the category of Chicano literature, is a nice complement to *The Farolitos of Christmas*. Susan Guevara's dark, bold illustrations depict animals in contemporary human clothing. One of the "cool" cats in the story wears a bandanna around his forehead, and a female mouse wears jewelry. Guevara's illustrations are great examples of elaboration and demonstrate how attention to artistic detail can add to a story.

Throughout the story, readers note that the cat, Chato, prepares a special dinner during which he expects to eat a family of mice he has seemingly befriended. The mice, however, bring a special friend to dinner and foil Chato's plans.

Even though flexibility is not obviously displayed in the characters of this book, students observe flexible thinking by analyzing the work of the author and illustrator.

Book Selections Containing Various Dialects, Languages, or Customs

Children enjoy the Spanish words in *The Farolitos of Christmas,* and it is valuable for them to hear additional stories that share words from other cultures. The wonderful books described below are written in Cajun dialect, Acadian-French, which is spoken in South Louisiana by descendants of people from Nova Scotia.

Lettres Acadiennes: A Cajun ABC by Don Goodrum (1992)

Like all good alphabet books, this one comes complete with marvelous illustrations that children enjoy. While reading the book, they find they must use the glossary in the back in order to figure out what many of the Cajun words mean. It is great practice for dictionary skills and even allows students to read the phonetic pronunciations provided.

Clovis Crawfish and the Orphan Zo-Zo by Mary Alice Fontenot (1983)

Fontenot provides translations of the Cajun words used in this story, and a pronunciation guide may be found in the back of the book. The story involves Clovis Crawfish and his friends, who save a little bird that has fallen from its nest. A moral dilemma is presented when Christophe Cricket cannot decide whether to help the bird since it will grow up and try to eat him.

Lettres Acadiennes: A Cajun ABC and *Clovis Crawfish and the Orphan Zo-Zo* are somewhat difficult to find but are available through Pelican Publishing Company, Incorporated, 1101 Monroe Street, Gretna, LA 70053. *Cajun Night Before Christmas* (Jacobs 1973) is more readily available.

Cajun Night Before Christmas by "Trosclair," edited by Howard Jacobs (1973)

The traditional story gets a unique twist when Santa drives a team of alligators pulling a skiff full of toys. Although the Cajun dialect is somewhat difficult to read aloud, it is well worth the effort for sharing this delightful book.

The Tickleoctopus by Audrey Wood and Don Wood (1994)

Students of all ages like *The Tickleoctopus,* a story including cave man language that can hardly be construed as cultural. This silly story tells how a boy and his tickleoctopus changed grumpy cave parents into playful companions. Small children sometimes pick up the idea of this story and create their own playground language during recess.

I See a Song by Eric Carle (1973)

Meaningful learning evolves as children realize that language is not the same in every country or area, and that people communicate in a variety of forms, including sign language, body language, mime, dance, and instrumental music. Eric Carle provides a wordless picture book in which he illustrates the phrase, "I See a Song." Vibrant colors suggest the movement and tones of a melody.

I Have Another Language, the Language Is Dance by Eleanor Schick (1992)

The author furnishes words and black and white illustrations that demonstrate the communicative power of movement. A dancer talks about how she feels the color of a flower and smells spring as she moves.

Tree of Cranes by Allen Say (1991)

Teachers can also supplement the lesson about farolitos with books about other cultural traditions. *Tree of Cranes* illustrates the Japanese art of origami, as a mother decorates a small tree for her son with paper cranes. This story has a subtle twist because this Japanese family actually shares the American tradition of decorating Christmas trees.

Tree Man by Carmen Agra Deedy (1993)

This story discusses the beginning of a Christmas tradition among South American rain forest animals. *Tree Man* is further described in chapter 3, "Originality."

The Legend of the Bluebonnet by Tomie dePaola (1983)

The Legend of the Bluebonnet has many similarities to the *Farolitos of Christmas*. DePaola describes an old Texas tale of a young Indian girl who saves her tribe by giving up her most prized possession, a special doll. The legend follows that the doll's ashes, which were spread over the land, became the beautiful bluebonnets that bloom in the hill country each spring. The comparison of personal qualities displayed by dePaola's Indian girl and the Mexican girl described by Rudolfo Anaya sets the stage for discussion of what young people can do for families and society.

PLANNING A NEW KIND OF GARDEN

Content: **Science—Plants—Environmental Destruction**
Creativity: **Flexibility and Problem Solving**
Critical Thinking: **Analysis**
Literature Selection: The Wind Garden by Angela McAllister and Claire Fletcher (1994)

Concepts in Book Selection

People face changes in life.

Age does not matter between friends.

Children can help solve problems.

There is more than one way to do things.

Ellie's grandfather lives at the top of a tall house, but he is no longer able to get down the stairs to go outside. Grandpa is sad that he cannot walk in the park or enjoy a garden; therefore, Ellie and Grandpa try to plant a garden on the roof of the house. Haplessly, the wind repeatedly destroys their seedlings and their dreams of beauty on the roof. Vivid illustrations in this book emphasize the power of the wind as it blows not only the plants, but also the hair of the characters. One unusual night, the wind picks Ellie up and carries her to a mountaintop where she discovers the many things that have blown away to the wind's garden. Colored streamers and other items blown away by the wind hang from the trees. Ellie borrows the idea and recreates the wind's garden for Grandpa to enjoy on his own roof. Grandpa's delight is a fitting reward for her efforts.

Ellie demonstrates flexibility when she realizes that what she sees on the mountaintop is a form of a garden. Grandpa also demonstrates flexible thinking when he accepts the wind garden, rather than clinging to the idea that a garden should contain only living things.

Lesson Capsule

This lesson is highly appropriate for a plant or environmental theme. Students learn about how environmental elements affect plant life through discussion or experimentation. They practice flexibility by thinking of alternative ways to create a garden.

Lesson Objectives

The students will

♦ identify and practice flexible thinking,

♦ examine the effects of nature on plants, and

♦ plan for protection of plants from harmful effects of nature.

Procedures

1. Help students understand that plants require sunlight and water in order to grow. This may be based on prior knowledge developed from planting seeds and experimenting with variations in the amounts of sun and water different plants receive. Make sure students consider extremes of precipitation, such as flooding or drought, as well as the effects of snow, sleet, and hail on plants. Ask students to also take into account extremes in temperature and wind conditions. Many students enjoy dramatizing the effects of the variations, rather than simply discussing them. Create two imaginary picture frames large enough to hold at least two students. Students demonstrate the positive effects of a condition in one frame and its negative effects in the other. If possible, use an electric fan to blow on students when they dramatize the effects of wind.

2. Brainstorm ways, if any, that people can protect plants from negative environmental conditions.

3. Read *The Wind Garden*, pausing before the girl follows the wind to its garden.

4. Discuss how the environment in the story causes trouble. Then, ask students whether any of the ways they brainstormed to protect plants against the negative effects of the environment would help with the conditions on Grandpa's roof. Ask if students can think of other alternatives for creating the garden. Could they build a sculpture garden, an animal garden, or something else?

5. Complete the book and point out how flexible thinking, which allows visualization of common things in new and different ways, might have led the students to consider making a garden from something other than living things.

Closure and Evaluation

Students write a brief description of flexible thinking, reflecting on times when they needed to use it. If possible, ask students to read their experiences out loud. Evaluate the students' understanding of the concept, based upon whether their examples are on target. Regurgitating the definition or examples the teacher used is not enough; students must apply the concept of flexibility to show clear understanding. When students have difficulty, ask them why they feel the incident in their example demonstrates flexibility. If they cannot think of an example from their personal lives, ask them to invent one for a book character or another person.

Personalizing the Lesson

Older or More Able Students

Students interested in science may set up experiments with plants to observe the effects of too much water, too much or too little light, or constant wind. Does constant wind affect the amount of water required by the plant? An electric fan can simulate wind, and the light experiment works well by keeping a plant under two lamps.

Students select one of these extreme elements and suggest a location in which the element would be a problem. For example, there would probably be too little light for plants to grow in a basement unless artificial light was added. And, a plant placed at the end of a house rain gutter drain would most likely drown when rainwater rushed onto it.

Students apply flexible thinking by brainstorming other types of gardens that could be placed in these locations. What is enjoyable and attractive, does not need light, and could be placed in a basement?

Younger or Less Able Students

Make a wind garden in a small area on the school playground or by a classroom window. The students use flexible thinking by discovering various items to put in the garden.

Related Literature

When the Wind Stops by Charlotte Zolotow (1995)
Zolotow's book is more appropriate for young children, preschool to second grade; however, it is a great story starter for older students. It describes natural cycles, such as the moon following the sun, and a rainbow following rain. *When the Wind Stops* works well as a preface to a lesson on sequencing.

Song of the Swallows by Leo Politi (1948)
Juan also builds a garden in this story, but it is a traditional type with plants and flowers. His purpose is unique, because Juan wants to attract swallows to live near his house. The story is about the swallows that leave San Juan Capistrano in the summer and always return in the spring. This book nicely complements *The Wind Garden,* as students think about the reasons both gardens were made. Both Juan and Grandpa wanted something beautiful to appreciate, and both worked hard to achieve their goal.

Miss Rumphius by Barbara Cooney (1982)
The wind plays a big part in helping the character, Miss Rumphius, spread lupine seeds across the land. This book is further described in Chapter 5, "Problem Solving."

BOOKS ARE FOR READING

Content: **Language Arts—Literature**

Creativity: **Flexibility**

*Book Selection: **Aunt Chip and the Great Triple Creek Dam Affair** by* Patricia Polacco (1996)

Concepts in Book Selection
Reading is important.
Watching too much television can be a problem.
Children can help solve problems.
Adults can learn from children.

The people of Triple Creek find that there is a high cost for watching too much television. Aunt Chip, the town's former librarian, "took to" her bed when the town built the huge television tower, but a child, Eli, helps her get up and fight for the right to read. After Eli learns to read, other children learn as well and gather books from all over town. It is obvious that the adults who found alternative uses for the books used both fluent and flexible thinking. They were not confined by the singular idea that books were designed for reading. The children find books hanging on fences, lying on top of roofs, used as door stops, and used as a dam to hold back water. When a special book is pulled from the dam, the water breaks through, flows rapidly, and destroys the television tower. When the adults protest, the children convince them that everyone should learn to read, and the young ones help their parents in this endeavor. In the end, Aunt Chip returns to her rightful place in the new library.

This book easily sets the stage for discussion of the fact that creativity is not always constructive. Although the adults exercised resourcefulness by finding alternative uses for the books they no longer wanted to read, they were actually destroying a rich part of life. It is highly important for students to learn to apply creative thinking toward the good of society.

Lesson Capsule

After examining alternative uses for common objects, students learn how books in the story *Aunt Chip and the Great Triple Creek Dam Affair,* were inappropriately used when the town's television tower was built. They discuss constructive and destructive uses of creative thinking, as well as the importance of reading.

Lesson Objectives

The students will

♦ exercise fluent, flexible, and original thinking by examining alternative uses of objectives, and

♦ examine the need for books in society.

Procedures

1. Ask partnered students to examine common objects and make a list of things for which they are used. Suggestions include an empty coffee can, a pencil, an egg carton, etc. At this point in the lesson, the students should be encouraged to think convergently regarding the real purpose of the objects. Students may share their lists in groups of four.

2. The groups of four then use divergent thinking to generate a list of alternative purposes for the objects, such as using the coffee can to store crayons or the egg carton to sort colored beads for jewelry making. Challenge students to think of as many realistic uses as possible. The students must think flexibly in order to break away from the boundaries set by the real uses for the objects.

   Intermediate Closure. Share the lists and discuss flexible thinking.

3. Read and discuss the book, *Aunt Chip and the Great Triple Creek Dam Affair.* Students need to acknowledge the reason the librarian went to bed when the television tower was built and why the adults created alternative uses for the books. Ask students to point out what the townspeople were missing by not reading. Possible answers include: learning about distant places they may want to visit; solving a mystery presented in a story; and enjoying the language and expression of a great piece of poetry.

4. Encourage students to make connections between the original activity they completed when listing alternative uses for common objects and the adults' uses of the books in the story. Help the students determine whether all of their answers were constructive. Discuss why all of the flexible thinking used by adults in the book was actually destructive.

Closure

Ask students to explain when to use flexible thinking. How would they use flexible thinking to save books from such a horrible fate?

Personalizing the Lesson

Older or More Able Students

1. This activity substitutes for the first two steps in the original lesson. Students question adults about things they used long ago that are seldom used today or are obsolete. Elderly adults often supply the best items, with possibilities that include manual typewriters, telegraphs, slide rules, sickles to cut grass, and so on. This also provides a great opportunity for research if students do not readily know the purpose of the objects.

2. Students list the original purpose of the items, as well as hypothesize as to why they are not used much now. They suggest ways the items might be used today, either for their original purposes or alternative uses.

3. Continue the regular lesson at the fourth step.

Younger or Less Able Students

1. This activity replaces the first two steps in the original lesson. The teacher provides each small group of students with three or four of some object. For example, one group receives four rulers while another gets four shoes. The students use flexible thinking by demonstrating alternative uses for each of their items. Consider using sets of paper clips, clip boards, coffee mugs, flashlights, and kitchen pans. Use items that have more obvious alternative uses for younger students. It is easy to adjust this activity for varying ability levels within a classroom by carefully selecting items for each group. This suggestion differs slightly from the original lesson because it requires action, rather than listing. Students use the objects to physically test various uses, which makes the lesson more concrete.

2. Continue the regular lesson at the third step.

Related Literature

The Library Dragon by Carmen Deedy (1994)

The librarian in *The Library Dragon* is a hilarious contrast to Aunt Chip in *Aunt Chip and the Great Triple Creek Dam Affair*. Deedy's librarian is a dragon, who refuses to let the children touch her beautiful, new, well-organized books. Even the school principal has difficulty reasoning with the librarian, Miss Lotta Scales, who actually sets the principal's tie on fire. The teachers attempt to talk with the librarian; however, nothing seems to work, and the children quit going to the library. Eventually a small girl, who cannot see very well, wanders into the library looking for her glasses and begins to read out loud. Other children migrate to the library to hear the story, and this warms Miss Lotta Scales's heart causing her scales to fall off. The new Miss Lotty creates an inviting library and things return to normal.

Additional Books in Which Characters or Words Show Flexibility

Big Band Sound by Harriett Diller (1996)

This book will show children the joy of playing with cans and other objects that people have thrown away. Sometimes, children can make a plaything instead of buying one at the toy store. When Arlis sees a drum set on television, she immediately wants one and can hardly wait to play her own set. She takes the initiative to find various objects that make interesting sounds to be her drums. This book would be a good primer in any classroom, for experimenting with sounds and making instruments.

The Purple Coat by Amy Hest (1986)

This colorful story begins as Gabby and her mother go into the city to visit Grandpa. While Gabby's mother goes shopping, she and her Grandpa enjoy sandwiches from the deli. When Grandpa offers Gabby a bit of his pastrami sandwich, she says she will stay with the salami that she likes. Grandpa suggests, "Once in a while it's good to try something new . . . How else do you know if you like it?"

Every year Grandpa, a tailor, makes Gabby a new coat, and every year it is navy blue. This year, Gabby wants a purple coat, but Grandpa is not sure that this is a good idea. Gabby uses Grandpa's own words, "Once in while it's good to try something new," to convince him to use the fabric she wants. Grandpa's creative idea, making the coat reversible with navy on one side and purple on the other makes everyone, including Gabby's mother, happy.

Little Cloud by Eric Carle (1996)

Eric Carle's idea for this book is certainly not new or unique. Most adults and children have spent time watching clouds, trying to determine what they look like, and enjoying their changing shapes. Yet, this book captures the visualization so beautifully, that readers become intrigued by each new shape as the cloud changes. The story depicts Little Cloud having the ability to see, think, and have feelings and seemingly suggests that this cloud chooses to become certain shapes. This demonstrates how people may try many different things in their lives and suggests that it is necessary to be flexible in deciding what to become.

It Looked Like Spilt Milk by Charles Shaw (1947)

This book is quite similar to *Little Cloud* and is popular with very young children.

Nimby: An Extraordinary Cloud Who Meets a Remarkable Friend by Jasper Tomkins (1982)

Nimby is a cloud with a special talent that often annoys his companion clouds. It seems that each time they decide to become a certain shape, Nimby becomes something different. For example, when the clouds fill the sky with white fluffs, Nimby forms a spiral. Luckily, Nimby locates a companion, and they make unique shapes together. This book differs from *Little Cloud* because it points out the figures Nimby forms.

Sam Johnson and the Blue Ribbon Quilt by Lisa Campbell Ernst (1983)

This book is set in early rural America when women wore long skirts and people rode to town in wagons. The women in the story shun Sam Johnson when he wants to join their quilting club and inform him that sewing is for women. They certainly do not want him to stitch on their quilt entry to the county fair.

Sam does not take this lightly and posts signs around the countryside calling for men's equal rights. The men rally and decide to make a quilt to enter at the county fair to prove that the women are wrong.

On the way to the fair, a gust of wind picks up both the men's and the women's quilts, and sets them down in a mud puddle. Although it looks like the quilts are ruined, Sam Johnson puts a creative idea into action and determines how to piece together the clean parts of each masterpiece into a unique new quilt design. His flexible thinking allows him to visualize possibilities in the patterns, rather than limitations. The real benefit of his ideas results from the men and women harmoniously working together to patch the new quilt.

Additional Lesson for Practicing Flexibility

Students practice thinking flexibly when they discuss the possible future consequences of problems or solutions. The sample that follows makes a nice warm up.

Out of Gas

On a comfortable day in October, the gas supply that fuels many of the houses and businesses in a small town abruptly ran out. Many of the people in the town did not even know about it as they relied solely on electricity; however, those who did use gas were very alarmed.

Students use Table 2.1, a matrix, to examine the gas problem from various viewpoints. Supplying answers for each category forces students to use flexibility as they project the consequences for various people in the town.

Table 2.1. Forecasting Matrix

	Immediate	Six Months	One Year
People who use gas in their homes			
People who do not use gas in their homes			
Businesses that use gas in their offices			
Businesses that do not use gas in their offices			
Manufacturers that use gas in production of goods			
Manufacturers that do not use gas in production of goods			
Manufacturers that use products made by others who use gas			

Books and Activities That Elicit Flexible Thinking

Sky Scrape/City Scape: Poems of City Life by Jane Yolen (1996)

Yolen collected poems from many different writers for this collection about city life. The poets write about skyscrapers and other buildings, commuters, graffiti, and many other things common to the city. The somewhat abstract connotations by some poets help capture the reader's imagination and simulate a very realistic picture of the city. The photographs of New York City were taken by the illustrator.

The poem, "Oil Slick," by Judith Thurman especially demonstrates flexible thinking as she encourages the reader to visualize rainbow beauty in a puddle of oil. Other poems in this collection give the reader a new slant, by suggesting analogies to normal city scenes and occurrences. For example, Christine Crow's words in "City Park" paint a pleasant, natural picture of buses and compares them to dragonflies.

Two Bad Ants by Chris Van Allsburg (1988)

The author-illustrator definitely used flexible thinking when developing this story. The entire book narrative as well as the illustrations come from the viewpoint of ants. This hilarious story describes the adventures of two ants who decide to stay in the kitchen rather than follow the rest of the ants back to the queen. Students laugh as the ants whirl in the garbage disposal, fly through the air when the toaster pops up, and get shocked in an electric socket. It is certainly worth reading aloud. Children under second grade, however, often do not find it as humorous, as this fantasy is plausible to them.

Short Activity

Students may explore the kitchen from a giant's viewpoint or take the defiant ants to another place, such as the bathroom, for continued catastrophes.

The Night I Followed the Dog by Nina Laden (1994)

The story angle used by Laden is definitely different and quite entertaining. As the title indicates, instead of a dog following a person, in this book, the person follows the dog. The illustrations show the dog combing his hair, dressing in people clothes for an evening out, and enjoying a relaxing evening with his friends. Unquestionably, the author used flexible thinking to concoct this book and its illustrations. In addition, the handwritten text is unique and interesting and demonstrates a creative form with which students can experiment. For instance, the word "eats" is printed in dark, wide, black letters with bites seemingly chewed out of it, and in the word, "exotic," the letter "t" is represented as a palm tree.

Two Dog Biscuits by Beverly Cleary (1986)

This book describes the relationship between twins, a girl and a boy, who are also great friends. The neighbor, Mrs. Robbins, gives them each a dog biscuit which they bring home to keep. Their mom insists that dog biscuits are for dogs and eventually takes them on a walk to find a dog that will eat the biscuits. Although they encounter several dogs, none of them seem just right for the biscuits. Eventually, they meet a cat, and the twins want to try something new by feeding it their biscuits. Mom, however, restates that dog biscuits are for dogs. The twins' idea works and the cat does eat the biscuits, suggesting that Mom should be more flexible in her thinking!

Chapter 3

ORIGINALITY

A child who uses original thinking to create a new toy or game is like a chef who creates a new epicurean delight. The chef wants everyone to have a taste of the dish, but the real joy comes when he or she sits down to eat it. Likewise, the child enjoys showing the toy to everyone but gains the most joy from actually playing with it.

Definition and Explanation

Originality results when something is created for the first time. A first-grader named Mark drew unusual things on his papers. These drawings appeared both on plain paper, completed when he had free time, and on spelling and math work papers. For example, Mark wrote his spelling list in road map form, carefully placing the words in random order about the page. Some words were upside-down, while others were written sideways. Although the child was not dyslexic, he also spelled a word or two backwards.

The teacher was intrigued by Mark's work. Actually, after grading 22 other papers, it was a welcome change for tired eyes! Unfortunately, two of the other students, also interested in Mark's new form for spelling tests, tried it on the next quiz.

Mark's spelling arrangement was original. It was different from any other the teacher had ever seen. It was also new and different for Mark because he had never before used this map form for a list. While Mark demonstrated originality, the two other children who reproduced his form did not. Although they used slightly different arrangements from Mark's work, neither of the other two children had originated this unique form.

The definition of originality given above sounds pretty clear-cut; however, adults could debate whether a child's picture is original. If children use a cardboard stencil to make an oval on paper, and one of them turns the shape into a clown, is it original? Adults have probably seen many oval-faced clowns, but has this child seen others? If the child has never before produced a clown from an oval or seen this done, the drawing is original for that child at that time.

Another way to think about children's work is through general comparison to the ideas of other class members. Did several students make a clown? If so, is it possible that this is general knowledge among children of this age, and, therefore, not original? If this is the case, but only one student drew a clown, the product could be considered more original.

Importance of Originality

Noticeable results of originality appear as inventions or improvements of existing products. Wrap-around flashlights, introduced recently, are an original improvement resulting from the need to hold the light in place, while having both hands free. These flashlights have long flexible handles that may be wrapped around hand rails or posts to hold them in place.

Society needs individuals who can develop original products that solve problems and make people's lives a little easier. Imagine life if no one had been original enough to invent the microwave oven. Many families would definitely be without supper!

Original ideas result from being able to change our patterns of thinking. Lawyers use originality to convince juries that clients are guilty or are not guilty, and surgeons invent original techniques for performing difficult procedures. The rapidly changing world necessitates the use of originality.

Examples of Originality

Adults

Readers can certainly generate their own list of adults who produce original works. Artists who draw or paint in a unique way, rather than creating a reproduction, demonstrate a great deal of originality. The same could be said of musicians, dancers, and writers, as well as previously mentioned inventors, surgeons, and lawyers.

Now consider a situation a bit closer to home. What do people who cook do when they have mixed all but one of the ingredients for a casserole, and then find that they do not have the last item? Perhaps they send the children next door to borrow it, or have a teenager, who is glad to use the car, go around the corner to the store. However, what if the person has just moved to a new city and does not yet know the neighbors, the children are gone, and it takes 35 minutes to make a trip to the grocery store? It's time to use some originality. Many readers have surely substituted milk or water for an egg, brown sugar for granulated sugar, or green pepper for onion. These are not necessarily unique; however, running out of powdered sugar and icing a cake with fruit yogurt may be. (Be careful! This cake needs to be refrigerated.)

People often use original thinking to solve other problems at home. A hair dryer works great to remove candle wax that a teenage daughter has accidentally spilled on new carpet. The heat warms the wax, which can then be soaked up with a paper towel.

Children

Youngsters are delightful when they unknowingly use original ways of saying things or use objects in new ways. Wooden spoons represent eye patches, flags, and telephones and have also served as wild horses ridden by proud cowboys. Long socks become dog ears, a rock is a bowl of cereal, and ice rubbed on cheeks creates the effect of a wintry day. All children use objects during play to represent other things; however, the less similar they are to what they represent, the more original the idea. A ball and an orange are similar in shape; therefore, this representation is not very unusual. A ball used to sit on as a chair is unique.

At times, teachers purposely look for original thinking by providing an opportunity for students to use it. When approximately 60 individual kindergarten students were asked how they could use a solid metal cylinder made by an engineering student, many of them said it could hold something down, as does a paper weight, or that it could be a wheel for something. Others suggested it could be a pencil or paper clip holder. These answers were original, but not outstanding, because the object looked similar to what the children had suggested. Several highly unique answers surfaced, however, and using the object as a Ferris wheel for ants was the most original. Although the metal cylinder was round like a Ferris wheel, the child had to transform the object by imagining it considerably larger and thinking of it as an open structure, rather than solid. The distance between these two things is much greater than between the cylinder and a paper weight.

Historical

Numerous historical examples of originality exist, and readers can make their own list by simply looking around. Televisions, automobiles, and tape recorders all resulted from original ideas. At times, the inventor generated the product by making connections between seemingly unrelated ideas or objects. For example, long ago in Scotland, a young boy had a rough trip when he rode his bicycle, which had metal wheels, over the cobblestone streets. One day, while watering with a rubber garden hose, the boy's father noticed the elastic resistance of the hose. An original idea resulted from connecting the hose and the tires and led to the development of a new type of tire (Gordon 1974). Other examples of inventions are provided in the explanation of the following lesson on *UGH* by Arthur Yorinks (1990).

Summary

It is reasonably easy for adults to value originality in artistic endeavors; yet, it is somewhat more difficult to appreciate it in academics. Often, concern with correct answers takes over academics, requiring a learn and recall format. Provide multiple opportunities for students to use originality in academic areas so they realize that creativity is not frivolous. At a minimum, students will use originality as they apply learned academic information to contemporary and future actions. Those students who learn to think originally and value their own unique ideas will enrich society's future.

INVENTING WITH *UGH*

Content: **Science (simple machines and inventions) and Language Arts**

Creativity: **Originality**

Book Selection: UGH **by Arthur Yorinks (1990)**

Concepts in Book Selection

New ideas are not always appreciated.

One idea can lead to another purposeful idea.

Siblings are not always nice to one another.

UGH parallels the fairy tale, *Cinderella;* yet it is set in the days of cave people. The main character, Ugh, is a young boy forced to clean the cave by older siblings. He finds his fairy godmother in the form of an inventor, who shows him a wheel. Ugh diligently works with the wheel, until one day his original invention, a bicycle, makes him famous. Unfortunately, the excitement of the cave people who see his invention frightens Ugh, and he runs away. The "foot for a slipper" episode in the fairy tale about Cinderella is replaced in this story with an expedition to find the person who can ride the bicycle. Eventually, Ugh emerges from hiding to take his rightful place as a boy King.

This story illustrates a character who uses originality in a constructive manner and is willing to take a risk. Ugh's actions also depict the idea expressed in one of the brainstorming rules, stating that adding to another person's idea is appropriate. A wheel is not much good unless it is used to create something.

Lesson Capsule

Students discuss inventions and discover that some of the present-day inventions were not widely accepted when introduced. After listening to the book, *UGH*, they will concoct original oral stories about other inventions made by cave men.

Lesson Objectives

The students will

♦ define the concept of originality,

♦ discuss Ugh's feelings following the invention of the bicycle, and

♦ practice originality by developing oral stories.

Procedures

1. Students discuss the term "invention," then brainstorm a list of those they use. Synonyms for invention include discovery, contraption, innovation, and originating. Inventions are new methods, devices, or processes resulting from study and experimentation (Webster 1995).

2. Depending on the reading level of students, the teacher either provides or reads information about several common inventions. The following are suggestions:

Velcro. These fasteners were discovered accidentally by George DeMestral in Switzerland in 1940 (Roberts and Roberts 1995). Following a walk in the woods, DeMestral had difficulty removing the cockleburs from his clothing and pondered why they were not easily discarded. Through close examination, he investigated what held the cockleburs to his clothing and developed this idea into a hook and loop fastener, later known as Velcro. Presentation of this example should include a display of various examples of Velcro usage, such as shoes, backpacks, and other items. Taking a walk in a field may produce a cocklebur for the display.

Rubber Tires. Long ago, a young boy rode his bicycle, which had metal wheels, on the rough cobblestone streets of Scotland. His father eventually helped make riding smoother when he used a rubber garden hose to create better tires. Dunlop used a common object, a garden hose, in a new and different way (Gordon 1974).

Resources for information about inventions include the following books:

Lucky Science: Accidental Discoveries from Gravity to Velcro by Royston Roberts and Jeanie Roberts (1995, 2) is a good source for information about inventions. This book encourages students to learn about science so they will be prepared to "take advantage of serendipity."

Martin Sandler's *Inventors: A Library of Congress Book* (1996) is appropriate reading for students, fourth grade and older. It is a valuable resource for teachers and parents.

3. Read the book, *UGH*, discussing the main character's feelings of excitement while he was inventing, his initial fears when the bicycle was discovered, and finally, the rewards for his originality.

4. Think about inventions other than the bicycle that use wheels, inclined planes, pulleys, etc. Invite students to work with a partner to tell creative stories about how these inventions were made. Students who have difficulty getting started might consider creating a silly cave man story about rubber tires.

5. Lead students to an understanding of originality. The following questions may help:
   a. Does an invention ever combine common objects or earlier inventions? (Examples follow.)
      • An electric mixer is an improved hand mixer with a motor.
      • Clothes washing machines have changed from a scrubbing board to an apparatus with a wringer, to today's automated machines.
      • A food processor combines ideas from nut choppers, graters, and slicers.
   b. What qualifies the new thing as a new invention?
      • Write the answers on the board for discussion.
   c. What are the characteristics of a *meaningful* invention?
      • Write the answers on the board for discussion.

Closure

Ask students to name things they would like to see invented. Discuss who might invent these. Ask them to explain how they would know if something were original.

Personalizing the Lesson

Older or More Able Students

Students dissect inventions to determine types of parts used. These might include clocks, toasters, fans, kitchen utensils, and so forth. A dissection consists of taking the invention apart and keeping a list of the order in which each component was removed. Screwdrivers, hammers, and various other tools will need to be provided in order for students to complete the dissection.

Finally, students combine the components of the inventions they dissected to create a new invention. The developmental level of students determines whether they actually build the invention or simply draw the idea. Drawing is usually preferred.

Extension: Put the original invention back together.

Younger or Less Able Students

Students examine simple kitchen utensils or office objects to determine the components of each. They list or draw pictures of the parts of each invention. Look at the following suggestions.

Simple Utensils
nut cracker
tongs
hole punch
tape dispenser

The drawing for a tape dispenser would include the wheel, the small bar to hold the wheel in place, and the cover.

Finally, students combine the components of the inventions they examine to create a new invention and draw the idea.

Related Literature

The Tickleoctopus by Audrey Wood and Don Wood (1994)
The cave man language and the pictures in this book fit well with the theme of *UGH*. This story is not about inventing, but it is about the origin of humor. It is further explained in Chapter 2, "Flexibility."

Inventions: Inventors and Ingenious Ideas by Peter Turvey (1992)
The first few pages of this book about inventions focuses on early humans from more than 1.5 million years ago. Students can view the types of tools they made for making fire, oil lamps, and other things. The remainder of the book provides interesting information about later inventions. Young children enjoy the elaborate illustrations in the book.

*53½ **Things That Changed the World and Some That Didn't*** by David West and Steve Parker (1995)
The title describes this book well because it contains inventions such as the toilet, the plow, the combine, and many other essential items. Students can use these as starters for projecting the inventions of the future.

STRANGE FRIENDSHIPS

Content: **Social Studies, Cooperation, Helping Others, Understanding Differences**

Creativity: **Originality**

Book Selection: Peach and Blue **by Sarah Kilborne (1994)**

Concepts in Book Selection

People who are not alike can still be friends.

Friends help one another.

Cooperation by groups of friends can do things that individuals cannot.

Living things have life cycles.

The world appears different from new perspectives.

Blue is a frog who is touched by the tears of Peach, a fruit who yearns to see the world. Unfortunately, Peach is stuck hanging from a tree branch and will soon be eaten. Blue enlists his 13 brothers and 15 sisters to form a tower that reaches Peach in her tree. After a slight mishap, Blue and his siblings help Peach sit in a small bowl they have made from mud, twigs, and lily leaves. Blue becomes her legs and takes Peach wherever she wants to go. As Peach views the world, Blue begins to see it in a new way, and their friendship becomes mutually beneficial.

The original thinking of Blue, who formulates the plan to help Peach and cooperates with his siblings to make a bowl for her to sit in, demonstrates how creativity can develop as a result of the needs of one and the compassion and thinking of another. It also subtly demonstrates that physical differences do not need to affect friendships.

Lesson Capsule

The students create a unique pairing by selecting one vegetable and one animal with which to work. They generate an original idea regarding how one of the two might help the other. Students create a story about the pair.

Lesson Objectives

The students will

◆ practice original thinking,

◆ explore anthropomorphics (Roukes 1982) in which vegetables and animals take on human characteristics, and

◆ learn to create a fantasy.

Procedures

1. Discuss friendships and the types of things friends do for each other. Ask the students if they know of any two people who are physically different from one another, yet are good friends. Such relationships may include people who have blond hair and those with dark hair, those who are tall and those who are short, and those who are physically challenged and those who are not. Link this discussion to an unlikely set of friends in the story they will hear. Read the book.

2. This book creates an odd pair of friends, as a frog and a peach get along together. Prepare a set of index cards with a name of a different fruit or vegetable written on each. Make a second, different colored set of cards with animal names. Students choose a card from each set and originate a way one might help the other. For example, a dog could loosen the dirt around the roots of a carrot so that the vegetable could get out of the ground. A grape could help a baby fish by serving as its toy. A kangaroo could carry a watermelon to the pond so it could get cool. (Children tend to do better with this activity than adults!)

3. Suggest that students create a fantasy story based on their odd pairing. This will be easier to do if the students first have an opportunity to practice creating an ending for the story that follows. The above example of the dog and carrot friendship leads to a fantasy story about the carrot who wanted to take a bath. A story beginning is presented below.

> Farmer Wilson always planted a garden behind his house. He and his wife enjoyed eating the lettuce, carrots, squash, and okra he grew. The neighbors enjoyed the vegetables too, because Wilson always planted too much every year. Some people thought he did this just so he could visit with his friends.
>
> Usually the only problem that occurred was when the neighbor's dog, Buster, got into the garden and tried to dig a spot in which to lie. Farmer Wilson would always yell at "that silly dog" and make Buster get out of the garden; but the dog was really sneaky and usually outsmarted Wilson.
>
> One particular year, the garden suffered because of a lack of rain. Farmer Wilson said that vegetables just are not as happy in dry weather. Little did he know that this was, indeed, a fact—his vegetables did have feelings. Carrots, in particular, were a very emotional bunch. Wilson never got wind of what actually went on in the carrot patch, but Buster certainly got a big surprise when he walked past the carrots one day.

Students participate in a group to create an ending to this story. For example, Buster might hear the carrots crying and start licking their wilted, green tops to make them feel better. Eventually, the children could describe how the dog digs up the carrots and carries them to the pond for a cool bath.

4. On their own or with a partner, the children write stories about the combinations they created in step 2.

Closure and Evaluation

While students read the stories aloud, the others comment about the original elements in each of the passages. Teachers judge students' understanding of originality, based upon the students' comments about other children's stories.

Personalizing the Lesson

Older or More Able Students

Add an element of research to the creation of original stories by writing the names of lesser known foods and animals on the cards students select. Suggestions include beets, asparagus, sugar cane, mangoes, and figs. Also, living things, such as crawfish and porcupines, add interest. Some of these require research to determine what they look like, where they live, and how they grow. Do not ask more able students to do the class-assigned activity as well as added research. When adding more difficult work to this assignment, such as research, students may work in groups, so their task is no more time consuming than that of their classmates.

Younger or Less Able Students

Allow these students to develop other original things that Blue could do for Peach. For example:

- What could Blue do to shade Peach from the sun?
- How might Blue keep Peach cool to make her last longer?
- How could Blue scare away birds and animals that might try to eat Peach?
- What would Blue do to feed Peach?
- What could Peach do to return Blue's friendship?

Related Literature

Tops and Bottoms by Janet Stevens (1995)

This book is not related to the theme of *Peach and Blue*; however, it is a great book to get students started thinking about vegetables that they could use for the Farmer Wilson activity of this lesson. *Tops and Bottoms* has a unique layout in which the fold of the pages is at the top, rather than the side of the book; therefore, the illustrations are top to bottom rather than side by side. The colorful pictures display various vegetables, which would encourage students to generate ideas for the lesson activity.

Tops and Bottoms is well worth reading aloud because it presents a humorous story of a partnership between a lazy bear and some hares who share a garden harvest. It shows the difference between root vegetables and others, as the hares outsmart the bear. When the bear barters to have the tops of the harvest, the hares plant root vegetables; and when he wants the bottoms, the hares plant only lettuce and celery.

Additional Books in Which Characters Depict Originality

The Gift of Driscoll Lipscomb by Sara Yamaka (1995)

This work describes the relationship between a painter, Driscoll Lipscomb, and his young friend, Molly. When Molly is four, Driscoll Lipscomb gives her a brush and a pot of red paint. Each year, she receives one new color. Finally, at age nine, Molly has all the colors of the rainbow and can paint her dreams. At the end of the story, Molly visits Driscoll Lipscomb, who is now an old man.

Barker's Crime by Dick Gackenbach (1996)

Mr. Gobble displays greed in this story by overeating and refusing to give food to Barker, a very hungry dog. Mr. Gobble also cheats people and is not popular in town. He takes Barker to court, saying that the dog is a thief simply because he sniffs the aroma of Mrs. Gobble's food. The people in the town support Barker at the trial, and the wise judge slyly enforces a unique punishment for Barker. The judge uses very original thinking when he forces Mr. Gobble to spend hours whipping the shadow of the dog. Mr. Gobble endures such frustration, fatigue, and anger that he leaves town.

Barker's Crime demonstrates the importance of viewing problems from varying perspectives in order to create effective, original solutions.

A Child's Book of Play in Art: Great Pictures, Great Fun selected by Lucy Micklethwait (1996)

Micklethwait selected pictures of original art for this book, which adults may use to entice children to look at paintings. She has sorted the pictures into groups and made suggestions for activities students may try with each. For example, students may search for games that children are playing in two of the paintings. She also invites them to pretend as they examine feelings depicted in another group of paintings. Several paintings particularly depict originality and are highly appropriate for class discussion, such as First Toothpaste Painting by Derek Boshier, which depicts a human figure inside a tube of toothpaste. Adults may also point out the original use of colors on the blue horses, yellow cow, and multicolored face in the book's other illustrations.

Students automatically use original thinking simply by thinking about each group of pictures in the manner suggested by Micklethwait. A creative teacher or parent will certainly find many more uses for this book.

Micklethwait also selected pictures for A Child's Book of Art: Great Pictures, First Words (1993).

Additional Lesson for Practicing Originality

All of the aforementioned books pertain to characters or events that model the use of original thinking. The following lesson does not necessarily contain these models; however, it is effective for guiding children to use original thinking.

HELP CATCH THE GINGERBREAD MAN

A Traditional Activity with a New Twist
Content: **Science—Animals and Inventions**
Creativity: **Originality**
Book Selection: The Gingerbread Boy **by Paul Galdone (1975)**
Alternative Book Selection: The Stinky Cheese Man **by Jon Scieszka (1992)**

Concept in Book Selection
Unexpected things happen.

Lesson Capsule

The teacher provides factual information about special attributes of animals. The students combine characteristics of two animals studied to create a new animal. They also apply the animal characteristics to a robot designed to help catch the Gingerbread Man. The sections of this activity are most easily presented on separate days.

Lesson Objectives

The students will

♦ gain knowledge about specific animal characteristics and how they help the animal,

♦ practice generating an original idea through combinatory processes,

♦ learn to enjoy productive freedom by participating in an open-ended activity that has no wrong answers, and

♦ learn the value of purposeful creativity.

Procedures—Activity Segment A

1. *Optional:* Give students several days to enjoy looking at nonfiction animal books or pictures placed in the reading center or other location. Displaying animal pictures on a bulletin board is also helpful.

2. Discuss at least eight animals with the class. Factual information should include the name of the animal and its special attribute(s). It is important for the children to understand the purpose of the attribute and how it functions. The information below may prove helpful.

> **Animals and Special Attributes**
>
> snow rabbit—white fur to camouflage it in snow
>
> turtle—protective shell
>
> snail—protective shell
>
> skunk—odor for protection
>
> kangaroo—pouch to hold its young
>
> frog—sticky tongue to help catch food
>
> porcupine—sharp quills for protection
>
> eagle—wings to fly
>
> spider—web to catch food

Beware if you use a skunk as an example. One group of students became so fascinated with how the skunk releases its odor that the author finally made a model of a skunk from a squeeze bottle covered with a fur hat. The skunk's reaction was imitated by releasing water from the bottle into a bucket. The children loved it! However, these five-year-olds later investigated a method to "fix" a skunk so it no longer posed an odorous threat. It took a phone call to the local veterinarian to satisfy these youngsters. To say the least, this is not recommended with older children!

Intermediate Closure and Evaluation. *Optional*: Students create torn paper pictures of the animals. Assessment involves determining whether the child can name the animal, its special attribute, and the attribute's function.

Activity Segment B

Acknowledgment: The following portion of the activity, which is used in many classrooms, did not originate with the author. Its original source is unknown.

1. Paste an animal picture on an index card or poster board. Prepare a minimum of eight of these, and then show the students all of the pictures. Take some time to name the animals and to talk about where the animals live and what they do.

2. Turn the animal cards face down and allow each student to pick up two. Make sure plenty are available, so that even the last child has a choice. The teacher may pick up any that remain.

3. Students discuss their two animals. Possible questions for discussion follow:

   What do you like about each of your two animals?

   What don't you like about each?

   Are there some attributes of one of the animals that would be interesting if placed on the other? If so, what are they?

   What new things could the original animal do with the new attributes?

How would the new animal look?

In what ways would you like this new animal better than the original one?

Possible responses from students include: placing the eagle's wings on a rabbit so it could more easily get from place to place; and giving a turtle the four legs of a tiger in order to get places faster.

If the group is small, each child may share aloud. Otherwise, students could talk it over with each other in small groups.

4. *Optional:* Students draw a picture of their new animal or rename it.

Intermediate Closure. Allow ample time for the students to describe their animals. Probe for details that encourage creative thinking. Help them expand their descriptions of the animals' abilities.

- What did you combine?
- Why did you choose to put these parts on the animal?
- What do you think this animal can do now?
- How will it use these abilities?
- *Optional questions:* What do think this animal will eat? Where will it live? What will be its predators?

Activity Segment C

Optional Business Setting: It is optional whether teachers use this segment as a simulation of the working world. The segment can be easily completed without having the class run as a business.

The class assumes a business name, such as The Development Company or Number One Designs (for first grade), and the children take "office spaces," complete with art materials, pencils, and perhaps desk nameplates. The group meets in the "conference room," located in a special place on the floor, to receive their work assignment. You may want them to report back to the "boss" (teacher) in written form, accompanied by a picture. A group of first-graders once insisted on wearing dress-up clothes so they were dressed appropriately for the office. They took the matter very seriously and truly concentrated while on the job.

1. Look briefly at the pictures of animals discussed above. Leave these pictures out where the children can refer to them in step 3.

2. Read *The Gingerbread Boy,* stopping at the part in which he runs away.

3. Explain to the children that they have been assigned to develop a new animal to catch the Gingerbread Man. Their boss said that they could create the animal any way they wanted; however, to design it they were to use special features from real animals. It is usually better not to model this or let students offer answers because, for this assignment, individual thinking is important.

4. Students go to different areas of the classroom as if they were working in separate offices at a business. Provide enough art materials so that everyone can develop an animal. Encourage students to use attributes of several animals in their reports.

5. Upon completion of the new species, students use a tape recorder to dictate to their boss the features placed on their newly developed animal, the real animals used in its development, and why these animals were chosen. How will each attribute help the new animal to catch the Gingerbread Man?

6. *Optional:* After all students have dictated information about their original developments, let the students share their creatures with each other.

Closure and Evaluation

Talk with students about the activity. After asking the types of questions listed below, it may be appropriate to talk a bit about creative thinking. This will obviously depend on the age of the children.

- What part of the lesson did you like or dislike?
- Why did you make the new creature?
- How did you get your ideas?
- Have you ever created an animal like this before?
- Point out that the students' work is original.

Table 3.1. Assessment of Work on Animal Project

OBJECTIVES The students will . . .	EVALUATION	YES	NO
Gain knowledge about specific attributes of animals and how these attributes are used.	Did students describe features on the new creature that were borrowed from real animals? Did they correctly explain how the feature was used?		
Practice generating original ideas through a combinatory activity.	Did students produce an animal that they had never seen before and did not borrow from another child? Did the ideas develop through combination?		
Learn to enjoy productive freedom by participating in an open-ended activity that has no wrong answers.	Were the students relaxed and having fun while making their creatures. Or did they often ask, "Am I doing this right?"		
Learn the value of purposeful creativity.	Could the students explain why they made the new animal?		

Teacher observations and the type of answers obtained during evaluation help determine the next action needed. A lack of answers, for example, often indicates that students require more preparatory activities, some modeling, and a great deal of group work before attempting individual work.

Personalizing the Lesson

Older or More Able Students

Students who feel they are too old to be interested in *The Gingerbread Boy* may enjoy working with a story about a thief that the police are trying to catch. They create animals or police robots to help outsmart the thief. It is easy to create an original scenario, and the students enjoy it most when the scenario includes names of businesses, streets, and familiar people. Perhaps the home of their own school principal was robbed!

Do not miss this opportunity to ask students to write their own episodes to accompany the scenario. Create a class book, such as, "The Secret Files of the _____ (name of your town) _____ (name your grade) Police Force."

Younger or Less Able Students

Choose segments of this lesson based upon the age and ability of students.

Related Literature

The Really Amazing Animal Book by Dawn Sirett (1996)

The text of this book surrounds the marvelous photographs of a variety of animals, while cartoon characters add an interesting element to the facts on living things. The editor arranged these animals into categories that include titles, such as Record Breakers, Animal Athletes, and Crafty Disguises. This book provides fascinating information about the animals, which could be used in a variety of ways, including in the aforementioned lesson about the *Gingerbread Man*.

What Color Is Camouflage? By Carolyn Otto (1996)

This nonfiction book, which is part of the series Let's Read and Find Out Science, provides excellent illustrations of animals camouflaged in their habitats. It informs readers why the animals need camouflage and can help students to learn more about animals in this lesson.

Who's Zoo of Mild Animals by Conrad Aiken (1977)

Children certainly get the idea of combining animals' characteristics when they view this book. They meet a rhinocerostrich (rhinoceros + ostrich), a guineapiguana (guinea pig + iguana), and many other unusual creatures. Small children especially enjoy the pictures, while older children like the lengthy rhymes that accompany them. Students like choosing animals to make their own creature.

Fishermen returning home without a catch for supper use originality when thinking of new stories to tell their spouses.

Chapter 4

ELABORATION

When archaeologists uncover parts of broken ancient pots in an area they are exploring, their important discovery is that people once lived there. However, they know nothing yet about the life of the people, what tools they used, or how they communicated. Without elaboration, the main message is presented; however, it lacks meaning without detail or explanation.

Definition and Explanation

Elaboration is the noun form of elaborate, which Webster (1995) defines as "planned or done with careful attention to numerous details or parts"; therefore, elaboration is the result of these actions. The application of the term elaboration to a discussion of creativity suggests that an idea has been embellished, developed, polished, or enhanced.

Importance of Elaboration

Torrance (1979) suggested that things need to be embellished before they become valuable. Teachers often ask students to clarify an idea or thought. Students elaborate on their original statements, and in the process add detail to their thoughts. The process of elaboration can also help students finish ideas that may prove useful in the classroom.

Questioning to retrieve details is helpful to parents especially when their children reach adolescence. Teenagers seem to take a solemn oath with peers that they will give parents as little information as possible about their lives. For example, a teenager and her friends were entering a voice contest held in a neighboring state. The girl told her parents that she was going to drive, take the others with her, stay at her aunt's house, and come home. The parents solicited more detail about the trip by asking pertinent questions. Following what the girl termed "interrogation," the trip became very organized and well-planned.

The type of questioning modeled by parents and teachers who are trying to get more detail about a child's ideas also helps students elaborate upon things that are not clear during instruction. Students ask pointed questions that usually elicit more detailed answers from instructors. Think about the number of questions that often occur the minute that teachers or parents give information about an activity. Students often ask things such as, "How long does it need to be?" or "Does my group have to use your markers or can we use our own things?" The answers help students construct the criteria for the activity.

Students also need to elaborate on any stories they compose. Teachers are pleased when stories have a beginning, middle, and end; yet, without elaboration, the passages may be rather dull. Help students refine the main idea in their stories by making them more elaborate and enjoyable to read.

Rudolfo Anaya, noted Chicano author, commented that writing is a lot of work. It is quite pleasant to initiate creative story lines and plots; however, he indicated that committing to the addition of details that make them meaningful to a reader requires a dedicated individual.

Examples of Elaboration

Elaboration also pertains to the development of plans and the arrangement of details. An elaborate host or hostess adds an extra flair to a dinner party through special details of the table setting or the inclusion of special music or lighting in the dining room. Individuals who plan meetings or workshops are elaborative when organizing the finer considerations prior to the gathering. These may include providing a lavaliere microphone for a speaker who has arthritis in her hands and cannot hold a microphone, ordering special luncheon plates for vegetarian attendees, and ensuring that the honored guest is met at the airport. Torrance (1979) pointed out that this elaboration is more than just organizing because "many details have to be considered and processed simultaneously."

Elaboration requires a group or individual commitment and a great deal of work (Torrance 1979; Mansfield and Busse 1981). An original idea may come suddenly as an "aha," but the development of it requires time and effort. Consider the number of great ideas that small groups of teachers produce in the lounge during breaks or at lunch. Few individuals or groups have the time to develop these ideas into organized plans, so the ideas die.

The act of elaborating brings great satisfaction to many creative individuals. Perhaps this comes in the form of embellishing words in a letter to a loved one or adding detail to the description of a comical episode in life. Some family stories grow better with age, as each new person who tells the story adds personal detail and style.

Young children delight in adding details to their make-believe simulations of life. For example, the portrayal of the evening meal may begin with a child pretending to be a mother cooking the meal while the other family members wait patiently at the table. The children add detail in the midst of the scene by asking the mother what she is cooking and then helping her decide the dish that is in the oven. During the meal, the children simulate real life through conversation. Try listening to their play episodes about families and note the elaborative language that the children may have previously overheard from adults.

The book, *Roxaboxen* (McLerran 1991), described in the activities section of this chapter, provides a wonderful example of children who create a make-believe world. They use elaboration as they add detail to their town with things, such as ocotillo (a cactuslike tree), to represent horses.

Elaboration comes with a price tag—the cost being in the form of fluency, flexibility, and originality (Torrance 1979). In a personal example, a highly creative first grade boy did not want to draw any pictures unless he knew he had plenty of time for the activity. He greatly enjoyed drawing tiny details and using rich colors in his art. When students drew pictures of their home, this student spent days detailing the individual bricks of his house. The completed piece was wonderful, and he certainly manifested the commitment and work ethic needed for elaboration; however, the other students completed many other drawings while he worked on one. It is pleasurable to note that the boy did not mind that the other students completed more drawings; he took great pride in the single piece he completed.

Summary

The world would be pretty dull without elaboration; wallpaper would be plain, clothing would be uninteresting, and literature would be rather boring. When students learn to develop skills of elaboration, they also develop the ability to make more detailed observations of their own world, adding joy and enrichment to their lives. The ability to elaborate also enables students to carry out plans due to adequate preparation and to embellish their efforts and actions.

Fishermen elaborate upon their stories about "the one that got away." Unfortunately, their elaborations often cause members of their audience to wonder about the truthfulness of the episode.

OUR TOWN

Content: **Social Studies and Language Arts**
Creativity: **Elaboration**
Book Selection: Roxaboxen **by Alice McLerran (1991)**

Concepts in Book Selection

Children are resourceful.

Make-believe activities are important.

One thing can represent another.

Children of different ages can be friends.

Marian and her friends create the town of *Roxaboxen* on an ordinary hill in Arizona. However, the place is not totally imaginary because they use found objects, such as rocks, broken glass, and old boxes to create the semblance of a town. The town hall, jail, bakery, and ice cream parlor are all important to the young inhabitants of *Roxaboxen* as they imitate real life by exchanging money, enforcing the law, and participating in wars. Characters in this story demonstrate elaboration as they enhance the beauty of the town by adding colored glass and other things to their originally plain constructions.

Lesson Capsule

Students hear a pared down version of *Roxaboxen*, written below, that gives little description about the town and how it was created. They ask questions in order to gather more information about the town. Later, students hear the real book, *Roxaboxen*, and compare the two versions. The lesson involves steps to guide students toward elaboration of basic sentences.

Lesson Objectives

The students will

♦ observe book characters' skills of elaboration,

♦ practice elaborating, and

♦ participate in asking questions that lead to elaboration.

Procedures

1. Read the following unadorned story about a town built by children. Gather the children in the usual class manner as when preparing to read a beautiful, elaborate picture book. Try to read the story enthusiastically but do not add anything to it. If

the students try to ask questions regarding story details, simply say that you do not know anything else.

> Some time ago, children decided to build a town. They built houses, businesses, and other things to play in. They also made streets and rivers in the town. The town changed often when the children added new things to it. They enjoyed playing games and pretending when they were in their town. They also took different jobs as citizens of the town. It was a great place to play and lasted a long time, but now all the children are grown.

2. Obtain the students' reactions to the story. Help them turn their reactions into specific questions about the short episode. Write each question on a separate card or sheet of paper and tape the cards on the board. If you have a computer in the classroom, connect it to a television or large monitor and type the questions on the screen. These question-writing techniques make it easy to categorize the questions later. You may expect some of the following questions from the students:

   - Who were the children?
   - How many children built the town?
   - What did they use to make the houses, businesses, roads, and rivers?
   - What kind of businesses did they have?
   - Who did the children pretend to be? What were their jobs?
   - What sorts of games did they play in this town?
   - What happened to the town when the children grew up?

3. Help the students sort their questions into groups. These should include questions about the following:

   - Children
   - Things Used for Building
   - Types of Businesses
   - Activities
   - Jobs

   These category headings may be used later for independent or group writing.

Intermediate Closure. *Optional:* Students may enjoy brainstorming possible answers to their questions or could be assigned to think of answers as their homework. *Optional:* Have students share homework ideas with the class.

4. Read the real story, *Roxaboxen*, by McLerran.

5. Discuss it in terms of determining the answers to questions posed earlier by students.

6. Compare and contrast the two versions of the story.

7. Partner the students, give each pair a sentence, and ask them to add some details to make the sentence more elaborate. Appropriate sentences include the following:

   - The children built a town.
   - They had different jobs and ran businesses.
   - Two children ate lunch in *Roxaboxen*.

- The children ran through town.
- The children grew up.

The procedure the students use to elaborate upon these sentences depends upon their age, writing ability, and what you want them to learn. Suggestions for various writing objectives follow. Please choose the appropriate one.

Objective A: The students will practice using descriptive words as a form of elaboration.

Ask students to embellish the existing sentences by adding adjectives. Note that students may want to rewrite these sentences completely; however, they must simply embellish each. The added details need not come from the book but may be created by the students. For example, the sentence, "the children ran through town," could become: "the lively children ran through the beautiful town as they rode their make-believe horses made of ocotillo."

Objective B: The students will practice elaborative writing by adding information that describes the topic sentence.

Ask students to use one of the sentences as a topic and to complete a brief paragraph that clarifies its meaning. An example using the sentence, "the children ran through town," follows:

> The children ran through the town. They often played this game of chase as they pretended to be fighting. They rode on horses made of ocotillo and made loud noises during the episodes. No one ever got hurt during these pretend events, but they had to be careful not to run into any cacti.

Closure

Reread the original, pared-down version of the *Roxaboxen* story; then ask students to share their elaborated versions of the sentences. Reading these in sequence creates a more elaborate story version. Help students understand and realize the importance of elaboration.

Personalizing the Lesson

Older or More Able Students

Ask students to determine objects common to Arizona that were used to build and play in *Roxaboxen*. These include the desert glass, ocotillo, and possibly the black pebbles. Then they brainstorm things common to their particular area of the country. For example, in the hill country of Texas common items might include old wood from barns, old fence wire, or wildflowers. Students draw how *Roxaboxen* might look if it were made in their own area or other parts of the country.

This work could be extended by using e-mail to contact students in other states who are knowledgeable about their environment. The exchange of *Roxaboxen* designs might also prove interesting.

Younger or Less Able Students

Students can actually construct their own *Roxaboxen* on the playground or in the classroom. An outdoor arrangement requires the designation of a portion of the school yard for the project so that the town can develop over several days. It is best if other students do not play in this area. Classroom construction may be life-sized or created at the sand table or sandbox. If the classroom does not have these, consider putting sand in a large shallow box.

The younger or less able students can also practice sentence elaboration by making a class list of descriptive words they hear during a second reading of McLerran's *Roxaboxen*. They add these words appropriately to the unadorned sentences listed above. This can be completed as a class project or made more difficult by asking students to complete the sentences independently.

Related Literature

The Year of the Ranch by Alice McLerran (1996)

Set in the early 1900s, *The Year of the Ranch* provides plausible background for *Roxaboxen*. After reading this book, students can imagine the origin of many of the objects used in the town of *Roxaboxen*. *The Year of the Ranch* portrays a family that fought the hardships of early desert life and features strong female figures.

Once fishermen have located fish in a body of water, they want to remember exactly how to find the spot again. They write elaborate directions pointing out the smallest of details about the spot in order to be able to find it again.

IMAGINATION STATION

Content: **Art, Science, and Math**

Creativity: **Elaboration**

Book Selection: **Dreamland** by Roni Schotter (1996)

Concepts in Book Selection
Dreams can come true.
Adults and children can share ideas.
Adults can encourage children.
Children can persevere when adults discourage them.

A young boy's dreams really do come true with the help of his imaginative Uncle Theo. While his family works in a tailor's shop, the boy draws sketches of wonderful machines and amusement rides that he imagines. Uncle Theo shares his world of imagination, but his father thinks they both have their heads in the clouds. When life becomes harder for the family, Theo leaves to seek his fortune in the West, but before he leaves, the boy gives his uncle all of his sketches. Later, when the family goes to visit the uncle, they learn that the sketches have come to life through the efforts of Theo and his friends. In *Dreamland*, people can ride The Spinning Machine or The Hoist and Spring, because a young boy dreamed and a man believed in the magic of imagination.

Lesson Capsule

This lesson helps students understand the elaboration needed for sketches used to build things such as furniture, small machines, and other things. Students plan and build a structure with different colored LEGOS; then they make detailed black and white drawings of the structure. Other students attempt to build the structure from looking at the drawing. Students listen to *Dreamland* and discuss the detail that must have been present in Theo's drawings.

Lesson Objectives

The students will

◆ practice making detailed drawings,

◆ learn the necessity of elaboration when drawing building plans, and

◆ practice communicating through drawing.

Procedures

1. Provide LEGO blocks or other simple building blocks and ask students to build something. If no type of blocks is available, sugar cubes work fairly well. The structure

could be something that already exists, such as a bed, tower, or building, or it could be their own new design. Encourage the use of many different colored blocks, if possible. Students should build their structures privately so that their peers cannot see the designs.

2. Ask each student to make a detailed drawing of the structure using pencil on white paper. They may not use color to indicate this dimension but will need to code it in another way. Explain that another student will be following the drawing, so it must be very detailed.

3. Students take the original structures apart when the drawings have been completed.

4. The teacher gathers all of the drawings and randomly passes them out. Students build a new structure based upon the drawings. They check each other's work and discuss any inconsistencies between the new structures and the original ones. If there are any problems, students should determine what other elaboration was needed on the drawings.

5. Students hear the story, *Dreamland,* and compare their experiences to the book.

Closure

Discuss professions in which adults follow drawings, diagrams, or maps in order to build something. Ideas below will provoke the discussion.

Professions that use drawings, diagrams, or maps:

construction workers, who follow plans for buildings

bridge builders, who look at designs for road or water overpasses

architects, who use blueprints for houses and other structures

surveyors, who use maps showing the location of roads and other landmarks

toy and game makers, who work from elaborate sketches

inventors, who build from their own detailed drawings

dressmakers or tailors, who use pattern specifications for cutting and assembling fabric

---

Encourage students to think of things they do, such as putting together a model that requires following a drawing. Lead students to the conclusion that elaboration is important.

Optional Writing Extension

Ask a realtor for written descriptions of houses that are for sale. Help students analyze the language used that might entice someone to want to buy the houses. After students examine these descriptions, ask them to write descriptions of their own homes.

Personalizing the Lesson

Older or More Able Students

Gather old house or business blueprints from an architect or builder. Large blueprints are preferred; however, if these cannot be located, pick up floor plan drawings where new homes are for sale. Students determine and list the type of information shown on the blueprints, as well as the code or abbreviations used. If interest is apparent, students may want to design something of their own, using their lists as criteria for their drawing.

Younger or Less Able Students

During the initial building activity, it is easier for these students to build with larger blocks of all the same color. Encourage them first to build something two-dimensional. Students may make a drawing of their structure on enlarged graph paper by coloring the appropriate spaces. Note that if the blocks are rectangular, the graph paper should also have rectangles; otherwise, the drawing will not look like the original structure.

Related Literature

The Way Things Work by David Macaulay (1988)
Macaulay provides wonderful drawings and illustrations that help explain how various machines work. Text is also provided for clarification, but most young children simply enjoy the pictures. These help students understand how Theo might have been able to build *Dreamland* from the boy's drawings.

53½ Things That Changed the World and Some That Didn't by David West and Steve Parker (1995)
This book contains numerous descriptions and illustrations of inventions. See annotation on page 44.

Inventions: Inventors and Ingenious Ideas by Peter Turvey (1992)
This book contains numerous descriptions and illustrations of inventions. See annotations on page 44.

A WAY TO REMEMBER

Content: **Language Arts and Social Studies—Map Skills**
Creativity: **Elaboration**
Book Selection: My Place **by Nadia Wheatley and Donna Rawlins (1989)**

> **Concepts in Book Selection**
>
> Things change over time.
>
> Memories are kept in many forms.
>
> Maps are important for many reasons.
>
> Elaboration is important in map making.

The back cover of *My Place* states that the book is like a time machine. Its author, Nadia Wheatley, is both a writer and a historian, whose words combine with Donna Rawlins's elaborate illustrations to create a book that children want to look at over and over again. The opening pages introduce readers to a particular area of a city in Australia and to Laura, a girl who talks about her family. Her map shows the details of the area, including where her friends live. A page later, it's 1978, and a boy named Mike tells his story and shows his map of the same area. Each new pair of pages carries the reader back another 10 years in time, until the final pages are narrated by a boy named Barangaroo in the year 1788. His map illustrates the natural state of the land, when people lived in huts and fished from canoes.

Each map shows a bit of the personality of the child who drew it. For example, in 1848, Johanna notes Mr. Owen's tannery and woolen mills on her map and writes, "Poo. They stink."

Lesson Capsule

Students draw maps of the playground or entire school yard. Later, they hear part of the book, *My Place,* and carefully examine its maps. The students apply techniques they learn from the book to their own maps.

Lesson Objectives

The students will
♦ practice elaboration using map skills.

Procedures

1. Take students outside and let them draw a simple map of the playground or school complex. It would be best if students do not color the maps at this time because they will be adding to them later.

2. Let the students gather in small groups to compare and contrast their drawings. Did everyone draw the map from the same angle? Did one person draw something that another did not think was important to include? Were there different ways of drawing the same thing?

3. Ask students to think about how the area they mapped may have looked 10 or 20 years ago. What might have been on the land before it became a school yard?

4. Share the book, *My Place*, which focuses on a specific area in Australia and contains maps of the location produced at different times in history. The book is lengthy, and students may not want to hear it all in one sitting. It should, however, be available for student perusal for several days before continuing the lesson.

5. Take comments from students about what they learned from looking at the maps in the book. What were the techniques the children in the book used to indicate various places or ideas on their maps? These include color, shapes, descriptive words or sentences, map keys, and arrows.

6. Allow students to rework their original maps of the playground using the techniques found in the book. They may decide they would prefer to map another area.

Closure

Display the maps and invite students to share what they learned regarding the need for elaboration on maps. Discuss how maps can help people preserve important memories.

Personalizing the Lesson

Older or More Able Students

Encourage these students to map the area where they currently live and to research information on how the land was used before the presence of houses or apartments. If this is not possible, students may instead project the future and draw a map of how the home area may look when the children are 100 years old.

Younger or Less Able Students

Denoting the proper relationship of things on a map can be difficult but may prove easier if manipulatives are used. Attempt to get younger children to show what things are located side by side or in front of another. If a sidewalk is available near what the students are mapping, draw the outline of the area and allow students to manipulate tokens, such as rocks, that represent the playground equipment. Ask students to place the tokens in the appropriate places. It is also possible to use string or rope to make a large outline of the area. Students can then stand inside the area to show the location of things. Embellish this idea by letting them hold signs labeled with the name or picture of what these locations represent.

Additional Activities for Developing Elaboration

Another Way to Say

1. Prepare students for this activity by asking them to write sentences about three different things they like to do at home. Put these aside for later use.

2. Choose a few elaborative sentences from various books, videos, or other sources, and display these for the children.

3. Ask the students to determine the main statement made in the sentences. To illustrate, ponder the following sentence from *Dreamcatcher* (Osofsky 1992): "Dreaming on a cradleboard wrapped in doeskin soft and snug a baby sleeps, smiling;" converted to simple form: a baby sleeps. Make a class list of the additional information provided in the original elaborative sentence. The list would include the following for the *Dreamcatcher* sentence:

   - *Where* was the baby? —on a cradle
   - *How* was the baby dressed? —in doeskin
   - *What kind* of doeskin was used? —soft
   - *What other things* was the baby doing? —dreaming and smiling

   The following are other examples of an elaborative sentence:
   Original Statement: "I listen to my sister's soft song, a song my father used to sing, and I think of my father's peach trees" (*Sami and the Time of the Troubles* by Heide and Gilliland 1992).
   Simple Form: I listen to my sister's song, and I think of my father's trees.

   - *What* kind of song? —soft
   - *Where* did the song come from? —my father used to sing it

   Original Statement: "I, in my nightgown full of stars, shivered with delight as I shimmied down the drainpipe to meet Ninny" (*The Last Dance* by Deedy 1995).
   Simple Form: I shimmied down the drainpipe to Ninny.

   - *What* was the person wearing? —nightgown full of stars
   - *What* was the person feeling coming down the drainpipe? —delight

   Original Form: "When spring rains came and the meadow turned to marsh, [c]attails stood like guards, and killdeers called" (*All the Places to Love* by MacLachlan 1994).
   Simple Form: Cattails stood and killdeers called.

   - *When* did this take place? —when spring rains came and the meadow turned to marsh
   - *What* did the cattails look like? —they stood like guards

4. After numerous examples, ask students to analyze the class list and create a short generic group of words that will remind them of questions

to spur elaboration. Students usually realize that the old standby *who, what, when,* and *where* questions help with elaboration.

5. Encourage students to create their own elaborative version of the simple statement in each example. "We walk along the sidewalk which sparkles with broken glass," from Eve Bunting's (1994) *Smoky Night* is first simplified to: we walk along the sidewalk. Students might make the simple more elaborate by writing about something else that could be seen on the sidewalk to create: "We walk along the sidewalk where the deep cracks weave paths in many directions."

6. To make them more elaborate, students rework their own sentences, from step one, using things they like to do at home. Ask students to tell the class which questions they used when adding to their own sentences.

Another Way to Draw

This exercise is similar to Another Way to Say, except that it involves a shadow or outline picture that requires elaboration.

1. Create a shadow picture by cutting out the body shape of a boy, girl, animal, or object from poster board. The shape can be manipulated more easily if a stick or ruler is attached to the bottom as a handle. Place the overhead projector behind a sheet with the light focused toward it. (Keep the light at a safe distance from the sheet, or it could catch fire.) Hold the poster board figure between the light and the sheet creating a shadow puppet that the children can see.

2. Ask the children to jot down questions they have regarding the shape's true appearance. If the shape is a girl, the questions could be about the color of the dress she is wearing, the color of her hair, whether she is wearing earrings, and other specific things about her appearance.

3. The children answer their own questions by drawing the shape and coloring the details requested by their own questions. Make a connection regarding how visual elaboration provides necessary information.

Additional Books for Developing Elaboration

A Child's Book of Play in Art by Lucy Micklethwait (1996)
This beautiful book is filled with pictures of original artwork produced by Vincent van Gogh, Edgar Degas, Auguste Renoir, and many others. Lucy Micklethwait has organized these into categories, such as Make the Faces, in which the paintings depict various moods; and Where Will We Live?, showing a castle, a country farm, a city apartment, and various other places. Students enjoy the artwork, as well as the questions in the book that will help them interact with the great works.

Leonardo da Vinci by Diane Stanley (1996)

Stanley has captured the life of da Vinci in both text and illustration. She discusses da Vinci's many notebooks that included sketches for paintings, plans for inventions, strange faces, and drawings of anatomy. Stanley adds an interesting touch to the book by using parchment-backed sketches, seemingly from da Vinci's notebooks, as part of her illustrations. Students who read this book learn that the life of this artist was not easy and that true fortune never knocked on his door. It may also motivate them to keep track of their own dreams and thoughts in a journal or notebook.

Chapter 5
PROBLEM SOLVING

Definition, Explanation, and Importance of Problem Solving

E. Paul Torrance's definition of creativity fully describes problem solving and suggests the skills needed to reach this higher-level goal:

> the process of sensing problems or gaps in information, forming ideas or hypotheses, testing and modifying these hypotheses, and communicating the results (Torrance 1994).

A problem is "a question or situation that presents doubt, perplexity, or difficulty or a question offered for consideration, discussion, or solutions" (Webster 1995). Problems are ever-present in the lives of adults and children. Early in life, preschoolers learn to say " I have a problem" and apply the phrase to everything from a broken crayon to muddy shoes. Adults spend a great deal of time worrying about their own problems, which range from how to get three kids to various ball practices on the same afternoon to devastating financial or health problems. The ability to solve problems is highly important and should be a significant part of educational training.

> Children can learn to view problems as possibilities, rather than as threats.

In this chapter, the discussion of problem types and problem solving methods is preceded by an analysis of thinking skills. These skills are vital to productive problem solving, and students need some degree of practice using them before jumping into a problem. Practicing thinking skills improves the chance of success during problem-solving episodes.

Higher-Level Thinking Skills

School curriculums often include the development of higher-level thinking skills, processes that require more mental effort than simple memory and recall. For example, many social studies guides denote decision making and problem solving (higher-level thinking skills) as key skills (Riecken and Miller 1990), which students use to solve problems. Higher-level thinking skills are sometimes known as higher-order thinking skills or productive thinking skills.

Treffinger and Nassab (1996) discuss productive thinking and define it as including "creative thinking, critical thinking, problem solving, and decision-making. . . ." They further discuss the fact that productive thinking "builds on a rich knowledge base, motivation, personal characteristics and styles, and metacognitive skills." The perspective of this chapter is that creative thinking, critical thinking, and decision making are all useful in problem solving.

Critical Thinking

Swartz and Perkins (1990) discuss critical thinking as "the critical examination and evaluation—actual and potential—of beliefs and courses of action." Numerous lists of critical thinking skills exist; however, close analysis of them often reveals similarities in semantics. One list of critical thinking skills (Maker and Nielson 1996) follows:

- determining fact and opinion
- choosing relevant from irrelevant information
- determining the accuracy of a statement
- determining the credibility of a source
- recognizing ambiguities
- identifying underlying assumptions
- determining external and internal bias
- recognizing valid and fallacious arguments

Goals of Thinking

Critical thinking skills and creative thinking skills, including fluency, flexibility, originality, and elaboration, contribute to successful problem solving. Flexible thinking makes it possible to move and rearrange components of the problem, and originality leads toward the development of something new. Children also look critically at a problem's components in order to know how best to combine them.

Problem solving and decision making result from a combination of thinking skills. In a recent interview, Treffinger suggested that these require both critical and creative thinking, and Swartz and Perkins (1990) concurred, calling these "specialized kinds of thinking." Students who use felt figures from different flannel board stories in order to create and tell a new story use both critical and creative thinking skills. Older students writing a new story combine characters or other parts of different books, as presented in the lesson, Crazy Stories, located at the end of this chapter. Both decision making and problem solving result in knowing what to do, and the thinking processes involved in both work together. It is impossible to solve a problem without making a number of decisions, including selecting possible solutions; deciding the criteria to judge the solutions; and selecting the final action plan. Conversely, when making a decision, it is important to consider many possibilities, think about the effect of each possibility, and then decide what to do.

Types of Problems

Years ago, problem solving in school was largely relegated to mathematics, particularly word problems. Luckily, the term, problem solving, now applies to a broad scope of problems in all content areas. Realistic problems for these areas can be derived from observations both inside and outside the classroom. Think about the types of problems that occur in the following areas and fields:

- science
- mathematics
- the arts
- communication

- politics
- construction
- social interactions
- spatial situations

The procedures for finding solutions to specific problems in each of these areas or fields differ significantly in type and method. For example, scientific problems often concern how to affect a change and may require the use of inquiry. On the other hand, some mathematical problems involve the use of a special formula to derive a single correct answer.

Although the problems and solution methodologies differ from one situation to another, each requires decision making. Therefore, educators need to teach children how to make good choices and to provide multiple opportunities for practicing decision making in a variety of contexts. Critical thinking is vital to making those choices because it makes children carefully examine the basis for their decisions. For instance, are the elements upon which they are basing a decision facts or opinions and does the information come from a reliable source?

Treffinger (1994) suggests that there are two main types of problems, real and realistic, and other problem types, discussed by Maker (1996), suggest there are those for which solutions may be generated or provided. These ideas are combined for use with young children, as illustrated in fig. 5.1.

Fig. 5.1. Problem Types.

Problem Types

Realistic
Problems that are plausible

Example: Suppose a child goes to the store to buy the milk his mom needed. When he tries to pay, the cashier says he does not have enough money. What should he do?

Solutions Provided
Problems for which a choice is made from the options given

Example: Should we study America's oceans or its rivers and streams next week?

Solutions Generated
Problems for which the possible solutions are generated by the problem solvers

Example: As a class, you may choose what you would like to study in social studies next week.

Real
Problems that occur and need a solution that will be implemented

Example: The school's electric bill is too high and each class is being asked to determine how they can help.

Both types provide practice in decision making for which students need critical thinking skills. Students should consider the basis, or criteria, for judging their choices, the perspectives of those affected by the choice, and other significant factors. Both types also open the door for creative thinking. People who think creatively are not necessarily stymied when presented with choices they do not like, rather, they sometimes generate and offer other ideas that may be a combination of the choices. If they do choose one of the original options, creative thinkers usually realize ways to use it to their advantage.

Thinkers who generate possible solutions for the second type of problem definitely use creative thinking by being fluent, flexible, and original in their suggestions. Critical thinking follows this period of solution generation when thinkers must make choices from their multiple options.

Problem-Solving Techniques

Creative Problem Solving

The Creative Problem Solving (CPS) process is a series of organized steps, each of which requires both convergent and divergent thinking. In other words, in each step, problem solvers think creatively as they diverge and generate numerous possibilities and then think critically and convergently by deciding which possibilities to continue pursuing. Solution seekers encounter the problem as a "mess," and work on it through steps of fact-finding, problem-finding, idea-finding, solution-finding, and acceptance-finding. Action toward solving the problem follows the last step (Parnes 1988).

The following brief explanation of the CPS steps uses a character, Grumpy Mrs. Smith as an example that starts as the following "mess."

Grumpy Mrs. Smith

The students in Mrs. Smith's third grade class at Utopia Elementary School have noticed that their teacher has been short-tempered since they returned from the holiday break. They know that Mrs. Smith has been having some back trouble lately, which she attributes to the large amount of "stuff" she carries to her classroom from her car each day. It is now February, and the children want the same easy-going Mrs. Smith that they had before the holidays to return to their classroom.

Fact-Finding. It is important to clearly state the facts regarding a mess. During this step, questions regarding the facts often arise and more information must be gathered.

Grumpy Mrs. Smith

The students listed various facts derived from the mess.

1. Mrs. Smith has acted differently since the holidays.

2. Mrs. Smith says that she has a backache.

3. Mrs. Smith says she believes her back aches because she carries heavy things from her car to her classroom.

After the students listed facts about the "mess," they realized that they needed to clarify each fact. For example, the students discussed the specific things Mrs. Smith does or says that are different and whether she acts differently all day or just at specific times. They talked about whether Mrs. Smith acts differently due to her backache and if her pain results from multiple factors.

Problem-Finding. Although the problem appears obvious in many situations, people waste a great deal of time solving issues that are mere consequences of the real problem. It is extremely valuable to take plenty of time during this step to determine the real problem. Restatement of issues in terms of "In what ways might we _____?" or "How might we _____?" helps clarify problems. Problem solvers need to determine the real problem and state it in broad terms.

Grumpy Mrs. Smith

There appeared to be several problems in this mess related to how Mrs. Smith can get her stuff into the classroom more easily, how she can remedy her backache, and how to keep her from being grumpy in class. Restatement of these problems resulted in the following:

In what ways might we help Mrs. Smith get her stuff into the classroom more easily?

In what ways might we help Mrs. Smith get rid of her backache?

In what ways might we keep Mrs. Smith from being grumpy in class?

The students decided that the real problem, at least for them, was "In what ways might we keep Mrs. Smith from being grumpy in class?" They wanted to state this in broader terms in order to provide more opportunities for solutions and eventually restated it as "In what ways might we remove our concern about Mrs. Smith acting differently in class?" This problem opens up the possibility for change in Mrs. Smith or others.

Idea-Finding. Problem solvers brainstorm solutions during this step and can use many of the idea-generating techniques discussed in the chapters on fluency and originality. Eventually, they narrow the field of possible solutions to about five, some of which result from a combination of two or more of the brainstormed suggestions.

Grumpy Mrs. Smith

The students spent time brainstorming solutions to the problem, "In what ways might we remove our concern regarding how Mrs. Smith is acting in class?" After generating approximately 20 different ideas, they chose the following five for further discussion:

1. Talk to the principal about the problem and get her to solve it.

2. Talk to Mrs. Smith about what they can do that will solve the problem.

3. Get a different teacher.

4. Accept the different Mrs. Smith.

5. Throw a big class party to make Mrs. Smith happier.

Solution-Finding. The solutions generated during the idea-finding step must be analyzed and evaluated in order to make a decision regarding which one to implement. During this step, problem solvers develop a short list of criteria for judging solutions. In other words, what must the solution accomplish in order to be successful? The criteria are stated in positive terms, in order to facilitate decision making. For example, a criterion about whether the solution is affordable would be stated as "cost-effective," rather than "expensive."

Problem solvers use a matrix to rate each solution on a criterion, assigning a number from 1 to 5, with 5 being the best. Finally, they derive a total of points for each solution and look closely at those that rated the highest. At times, the highest rated idea is not used, or it has parts of other solutions added to it. The matrix serves as a guide for deciding what solution to use but does not have to be the final word.

Grumpy Mrs. Smith

Mrs. Smith's students used the following criteria for evaluating their solutions:

- students feel good in class
- good for Mrs. Smith
- cost-effective
- possible
- can be done at school

The students evaluated each suggested solution, according to the criteria using a rating of 1 to 5, with 5 being the most positive. They used a matrix (see Table 5.1) to make things easier.

Table 5.1. Problem-Solving Matrix

Solution	students feel good in class	good for Mrs. Smith	cost-efficient	is possible	done at school	Total
talk to principal	3	1	5	5	5	19
talk to Mrs. Smith	3	2	5	5	5	20
get a different teacher	3	1	5	1	5	15
accept the different Mrs. Smith	1	4	5	1	5	16
throw a class party	1	4	1	3	5	14

The students' matrix work indicated that their best options were to either talk with the principal or talk with Mrs. Smith. They were concerned that if they talked to the principal, Mrs. Smith might get grumpier, because she might get into trouble; so ultimately, the students decided to talk with Mrs. Smith.

Acceptance-Finding. The final step in CPS is critical because it involves planning for implementation of the determined solution. This may involve how to contact important parties, what to say during a meeting, or where to obtain supplies required for the solution.

Grumpy Mrs. Smith

The students needed to figure out just exactly how to approach Mrs. Smith. They did not want to hurt her feelings, cause her trouble, or make the situation worse. They discussed an appropriate time to have the discussion, the students who should speak to her, what to say and how to say it, as well as what to do if the confrontation did not go well. After working out all the necessary details, a small group of students composed a letter asking Mrs. Smith to hold a class meeting to discuss an important class issue. Later, they asked Mrs. Smith for a meeting time and reported it to the rest of the students. The three students designated to do the talking got together and wrote down what each of them would say. Mrs. Smith listened carefully to the students and made a few suggestions regarding what they could do to help her. She also promised to go to the doctor about her backache and to try to be "herself." She actually appreciated their concern and the whole class felt closer after the meeting.

Contemporary Creative Problem Solving

At a 1996 workshop, Treffinger and others suggested a contemporary model of CPS, in which the order of steps can be altered and some eliminated for specific problems. Consider types of problems for which the solution options are provided. It is also possible that only the solution-finding step would be needed, while problems that require generation of options require more steps. Problem solvers may need to consider criteria for evaluating when they attempt to determine the real problem. Specifically, children should think about what problem they can actually solve, as opposed to those which are beyond their control.

Treffinger (1994) notes three stages in the CPS model and lists the components of each stage.

Understanding the Problem

- Mess-Finding
- Data-Finding
- Problem-Finding

Generating Ideas

- Idea-Finding

Planning for Action

- Solution-Finding
- Acceptance-Finding

Young children, at least as young as kindergarten age, are capable of successfully using CPS. Early childhood instructors will find better success when they use pictures or objects to represent the components of CPS. Experts (Puccio, Keller-Mathers, and Treffinger 1997) who use CPS with young children, suggest the following analogies for each CPS step as a way to remind younger students about the tasks.

Mess-finding is like a cleaner.

Data-finding is like a detective.

Problem-finding is like a doctor.

Idea-finding is like a collector.

Solution-finding is like an inventor.

Acceptance-finding is like a salesperson.

In a 1996 workshop, Keller-Mathers indicated that allowing students to don the clothing representative of each occupation and to explore the tools of each job increases their understanding of the CPS steps. Pictures of a person represented in each analogy stimulate student recall of the component.

It is helpful for teachers to analyze the steps they currently use for problem solving in the classroom. Teachers usually realize that they are already applying some of the components of CPS and that others could easily be added for more productive solution-finding. The final component, acceptance-finding, provides instructors with an avenue for working on social skills, tactfulness, and other things important for building students' character.

Use of Children's Literature for Problem Solving

Children's literature allows students to experience real-life situations vicariously. They read about many types of problems and observe differences in the way characters approach and solve them. It is healthy for children to realize that problems are simply a part of life and that it is important to develop coping skills for maintaining personal survival while working out solutions. When children read about problems similar to their own, they feel less alone. Specific children's books described in this chapter discuss real issues, including wanting to be noticed or to gain attention, seeking personal rights and freedoms, and wishing others would leave personal possessions alone.

Meador (1992a) used children's literature to help kindergarten students practice problem-solving skills. She guided the children in using some of the steps in the aforementioned Creative Problem Solving process, asking for metaphoric thinking when appropriate. Meador used Wanda Gag's (1941) book,

Nothing at All, which is currently out of print but can be located in many libraries. (*Harry the Dirty Dog* [Zion 1956] is an appropriate substitution for this problem-solving exercise.) *Nothing at All* is about three dogs, two of which are discovered and taken home by a girl and a boy. Unfortunately, the third dog is invisible, so the children do not put him in their wagon for the journey home. The following questions guided the discussion and served as steps in the problem-solving process. The actual problem-solving steps, such as problem-finding, idea-finding, and solution-finding, were not identified for the students; they simply answered questions.

Mess-Finding
This is presented as the first part of the story.

Fact-Finding
1. What do we actually know about this mess?

Problem-Finding
2. What is the problem in this story?

Idea-Finding
3. What do you think should happen to correct the problem?
4. What can we compare to this problem?
5. What helped in that situation?
6. What ideas can we borrow from that situation?
7. Do you have any other ideas?

Solution-Finding
8. How will we know if our idea works?
9. Which of our ideas will work the best?
10. How will the story end if the author uses our idea?

The kindergarten students participating in the problem-solving session made specific decisions during each step of the process. Students used divergent thinking first to generate many ideas, and then used critical thinking to focus their thoughts.

1. *What do we actually know about this mess?*
   The children discussed the fact that two dogs had been taken home by the children and one dog had been left behind. They knew that the dog left behind was invisible and that he also wanted to go with the children.

2. *What is the problem in this story?*
   The five-year-olds decided that the real problem was that the invisible dog wanted to be noticed and loved. Instead of spending time deciding how to make the dog visible, they worked on this problem.

3. *What do you think should happen to correct the problem?*
   Initially, some of the young students suggested solutions that would make the dog visible, such as painting him and putting water or shampoo on him. When students recalled the real problem they were trying to solve, they suggested other solutions: The dog could make shadows, he could find an invisible man to see him, or he might splash

in the water and hope someone would see the movement. One student thought the children would notice the "doggy smell" or see his footprints (Meador 1994).

4. *What can we compare to this problem?*

    Meador asked the children to compare the dog's situation of wanting to be noticed to a situation in which a child was separated from parents or adult friends at the mall. This comparison helped students to think metaphorically and to recall any prior experiences that apply to this problem-solving situation. The children eagerly discussed times when they had been lost or had seen other children in distress.

5. *What helped in that situation?*

    Students stated that it was good to find a policeman, stand on something tall and look around, find a microphone to talk into, or simply yell. ("Yo, Mom!" seemed to be the preferred phrase to holler.)

6. *What ideas can we borrow from that situation?*

    When students were asked how the solution to being lost could be used in the invisible dog problem, they realized that the dog needed to bark so the children would become aware of him.

7. *Do you have any other ideas?*

    Some students thought of additional solutions during discussion and needed plenty of opportunities to express them.

    Note: The kindergarten students were satisfied and felt their problem-solving session was complete; therefore, the final steps of the process were not used with this group. It is possible that the other steps could be discussed on another day or at a different time. The conclusion of the process, which follows, should be used with older students, if appropriate.

8. *How will we know if our idea works?*

    Students would probably know that if the children in the story noticed the dog, they had already solved the problem. They might also think it was important for the children to take the invisible dog home.

9. *Which of our ideas will work the best?*

    After choosing three or four favorite solutions, the children could discuss whether each solution would meet the criteria established during solution-finding. It is difficult for young students to agree on a single solution, especially if there are only two criteria. The essential point is that the students will exercise critical thinking when talking about options based on criteria.

10. *How will the story end if the author uses our idea?*

    Students enjoy finishing the book with their own solution that they present orally, dramatically, or in writing. Kindergarten students enjoy tape-recording their stories, which prove to be welcome additions to the listening center.

Questioning Strategies

Adults are good facilitators of the problem-solving process if they know how to ask appropriate questions and refrain from interjecting their own ideas. This skill is not only vital for problem solving, but for most interactions; teachers who make a difference know how to ask the right questions. Rather than querying about facts and details in a literature selection, they pose questions that initiate various types of student thinking.

Timely questions guide the problem-solving process and give students the autonomy to practice thinking without risk of failure. Riecken and Miller (1990) suggest focus questions for problem solving. A few of these follow:

What is the problem here?

Why is it a problem?

For whom is it a problem?

How might she (the story character) solve this problem?

What would you do if you were in this situation?

Does he (the story character) have to make a decision here?

What do you think his options are?

Are some of his options better than others? Why?

Some adults who make a conscious effort to ask children different types of questions find that specific strategies can be effective. One of these, Six Thinking Hats, developed by Edward de Bono (1985) provides a framework for developing different types of thinking and is appropriate to use when facilitating problem solving. Once teachers understand the type of thinking represented by each of the colored hats, they ask questions formulated to encourage reasoning. Consider the following example based on Maurice Sendak's (1963) book *Where the Wild Things Are*. Descriptions of the hats were obtained from de Bono's (1991) *Six Thinking Hats for Schools*.

White Hat: information, facts—What did Max's mother do at night after he made mischief all day?

Red Hat: feelings, emotions, opinions—What feelings would you have if you were sent to bed without any supper?

Black Hat: judgment, negative elements—What, if any, were the negative things that happened because Max was mischievous?

Yellow Hat: benefits, positive side—What was a good thing that happened to Max when he visited the Wild Things?

Green Hat: creativity—What else might Max have done while he was King of the Wild Things?

Blue Hat: directing thinking—What type of thinking should Max have used before his mother became upset with him? Why?

Six Thinking Hats is also an appropriate questioning framework for problem solving and particularly helps guide students toward analysis of solutions. Some teachers rely on small colored strips of paper, which they hold in their hands while questioning students. After asking a question calling for a specific type of thinking, teachers remove its representative color from those they are holding. This also helps avoid overuse of any certain type of question. Questions that follow are typical of those used in problem-solving sessions. Any colored hat question may be used in the various components of problem solving; therefore, those suggested below serve merely as examples.

White Hat: information, facts—Who is having a problem? What information do you have about the problem? (Fact-finding)

Red Hat: feelings, emotions, opinions—Are there any specific feelings, emotions, or opinions that contribute to the problem? (Fact-finding)

Black Hat: judgment, negative elements—What bad things are happening because of this problem? (Fact-finding) What are the negative points of each of the solutions suggested? (Solution-finding)

Yellow Hat: benefits, positive side—Are any good things happening because of this problem? (Fact-finding) What are the benefits of each of the solutions suggested? (Solution-finding)

Green Hat: creativity—What are possible solutions to the problem? (Idea-finding) How can you modify the suggested solutions to make them more effective? (Idea-finding, Solution-finding, Acceptance-finding)

Blue Hat: directing thinking—Can you suggest a way that we should think about this? (All components)

Summary

Think what life would be like if everyone viewed problems as opportunities. Children who learn to solve problems during their years in school gather the techniques and tools that will help them approach problems with this attitude. Adults who model problem solving, rather than displaying desperation regarding the "downs" of life, help children to remain optimistic about their future.

SAVING THE BIRDS

Content: **Social Studies/Women's Rights and Science/Birds—Extinction**

Creativity: **Problem Solving**

Book Selection: She's Wearing a Dead Bird on Her Head! **by Kathryn Lasky (1995)**

> **Concepts in Book Selection**
>
> People need to protect the living things in the environment.
>
> Cooperation is important to solving a problem.
>
> Planning is important to solving a problem.
>
> Both women and men can influence change.

The vivid illustrations and text included in this book make it somewhat comical; however the subject is very serious. The story, set in Boston around 1896, informs readers about the lack of women's rights; yet portrays the power, determination, and success of a group of women in a club known as the Audubon Society. The story begins when two women start noticing the large number of fashionable women wearing feathers, bird wings, and even dead birds on their hats. They garner support from other women, children, and their husbands who have the power to vote and go to public places, such as Congress and the state legislature.

The women display problem-solving skills when they need to obtain the name of the business illegally supplying hat makers with the birds and feathers. In a well-planned adventure to New York, two of the women pose as fashionable ladies, purchase two hats, and find out the name of the unscrupulous supplier. The law takes over, and the birds are protected.

This story offers a wonderful model of how creative ideas often succeed due to the careful planning of those involved. It was absolutely necessary at that time for the women to involve men in their organization because without them they would have been unable to get the legislative support required for the laws to protect the birds.

She's Wearing a Dead Bird on Her Head! is a good book demonstrating that determination is a personality characteristic of many creative individuals. It also provides an opportunity for adults to discuss how a great idea could go awry if problem solvers do not use common sense. It is also vital that students learn they cannot simply muscle their ideas into society.

Lesson Capsule

Students consider the solutions used in the book when generating ideas for solving other problems.

Lesson Objectives

The students will

♦ become aware of the importance of finding acceptance for new ideas, and

♦ practice writing persuasive letters or advertisements.

Procedures

1. Check current events to determine if there are any controversial issues that would interest the students. In the past these included the killing of large numbers of wolves that were threatening livestock, riots in California, and allowing people in some states to carry concealed weapons. It may be more appropriate to discuss whether students should wear uniforms to school, whether it should be mandatory for all students to ride the bus in order to avoid the school traffic jam, or other topics of immediate interest to children.

2. Allow students to discuss one of the issues, making sure they produce a class chart of both the pros and the cons of their problem's solutions. As a class, decide which person or persons must be convinced in order for the students' side of the issue to prevail.

3. Cooperative groups then brainstorm ways to convince the appropriate persons to support the students' side of the issue. Groups should record their suggestions for later use. *Note:* This is a good point for a break in the lesson, if needed.

4. Tell students they will hear a story about how a group of people managed to gain support for their side of an issue. Read *She's Wearing a Dead Bird on Her Head!* Discuss the steps the women took to organize for action. Be sure students notice the importance of involving someone with authority and influence in the plan.

5. Allow the groups to return to work on their plans for the class issue being discussed, and encourage them to borrow ideas from *She's Wearing a Dead Bird on Her Head!* if possible. *Optional:* Students often enjoy creating a billboard advertising their side of the issue.

6. Each student group presents its ideas to the class. It is fun when the groups dramatize their plans. Suggest that they use some type of visual aid or manipulative in the presentation.

7. *Writing Extension:* Individuals write letters to a friend using the ideas developed by the group. Students try to persuade the friend to take their side of the issue.

Closure

Discuss the reason it is important to get support for an issue. Explain that it is important to seek support for creative ideas or inventions. When something is new and unique, the public does not always readily accept it. Students need to plan how they will introduce creative ideas.

Personalizing the Lesson

Older or More Able Students

Students prepare a speech, which could be made to the school board, regarding one of the controversial educational issues listed above. Students present their speeches to an administrator in the elementary school. They will need to practice their speeches with one another before the final presentation.

Younger or Less Able Students

Students discuss the threatened extinction of another animal such as the manatee. This allows more direct connection to the book and its solution.

Related Literature

Have You Seen Birds? by Joanne Oppenheim and Barbara Reid (1968)
    The interesting illustrations in this book, made from a clay substance, allow children to see the different colors and types of feathers birds have. This helps children understand what might be attractive about decorating hats with them. The text of the book is very simple and composed in rhyme.

Fishermen must problem-solve when the bait or lure they are presenting does not get the attention of the fish. They peer into their tackle boxes, examine numerous possibilities, and make decisions about what new bait to offer the fish.

DUCK SAFE

Content: **Science and Language Arts**
Creativity: **Problem Solving**
Book Selection: ***Farmer Schultz's Ducks*** **by Colin Thiele (1986)**

Concepts in Book Selection

People must protect animals.

People can destroy animal life.

Perseverance is important when solving a problem.

People can learn from solutions that do not work.

The ducks on Farmer Schultz's farm are among the most beautiful in South Australia, and each day they waddle from the backyard, across the road, and down to the river. At first, cars always stop and wait for the ducks to cross, but as the traffic increases, drivers are less patient.

The story tells of the many different solutions Farmer Schultz and his family try to help the ducks go safely across the road. They use signs to caution drivers about the duck crossing, and when this fails, the family builds a high ramp over the road for the ducks to use. When disaster collapses the duck-laden ramp, Farmer Schultz lays a pipe under the road so the ducks can safely get to the water. The book illustrates problem solving, flexible thinking, and determination.

Lesson Capsule

Students brainstorm solutions to a problem presented in the book and categorize their ideas. They discuss the importance of thinking from a variety of perspectives.

Lesson Objectives

The students will

◆ practice brainstorming solutions to problems,

◆ recognize solution categories, and

◆ develop criteria for judging problem solutions.

Procedures

1. The book, *Farmer Schultz's Ducks*, logically falls into sections designated by each new solution and its failure. Children enjoy brainstorming between each segment, thinking of what they might do next if they were Farmer Schultz. Write the brain-stormed solutions from each segment on the board or on a chart for later use. Include

the solutions that Farmer Schultz tried. The following suggestions serve as examples of student answers.

Create a billboard to warn drivers.

Have radio announcements about the problem.

Take turns standing by the road with a sign to tell drivers to slow down.

Keep the ducks on the water side of the road.

Ask the police for help.

Get the city to move the road.

Give the ducks away.

---

3. After reading the story, ask students to help group the listed solutions into categories. The following box lists plausible categories for the above examples.

Things for drivers to see

Things for drivers to hear

Things the farmer can do

Things other people can do

---

4. Use the categorical information to illustrate to students that in order to solve problems, it is important to look for solutions from a variety of perspectives in various categories. Encourage the use of this information by developing a question or two that students can recall when working on a problem. Appropriate questions include, "How can I think about this problem from another angle?" and "How would an expert solve this problem?"

Closure

Point out that good solutions are not always successful, as in Farmer Schultz's story. But, it is important to persevere.

Extension 1

Add category headings that the students have not yet used and ask them to think of solutions for each classification. Think about using categories, such as things the animals could do, solutions that could be created with water, and solutions that require mechanical objects.

Extension 2

Students design a billboard to caution drivers about the ducks.

Extension 3

Students write a mock formal letter to city hall requesting that they move the road or to the police chief asking for an officer to guard the duck crossing.

Personalizing the Lesson

Older or More Able Students

Some students feel that this book is somewhat childish and uninteresting, largely due to the fact that it is about ducks. Help them realize that it is being used simply for illustrating problem solving. Suggest that students change the story more to their liking prior to completing the lesson. They might use another animal, a different location, or another circumstance. Perhaps people and their dogs in a city are attempting to get across a busy street from the parking lot to the dog obedience school that has scheduled a class during rush hour. Students may use the same solutions as Farmer Schultz.

Younger or Less Able Students

It is best for the teachers to list categories and ask students to group their brainstormed solutions according to these. This is simpler for them than trying to designate the category headings.

Related Literature

Make Way for Ducklings by Robert McCloskey (1941)
McCloskey's award winning story describes a family of ducks in Boston who had to cross a busy city street. It is a nice contrast to the story of *Farmer Schultz's Ducks*, which is set in the country.

CRAZY STORIES

Content: **Language Arts**

Creativity Goal: **Problem Solving and Originality**

Book Selections: **Where the Wild Things Are by Maurice Sendak (1963)**

Two Bad Ants by Chris Van Allsburg (1988)

Tacky the Penguin by Helen Lester (1988)

Fly Away Home by Eve Bunting (1991)

Note: The lesson that follows uses the books listed above; however, any book that the children have read may be used for making the story matrix.

Lesson Capsule

After the students read or listen to several books over a period of time, they supply components of each to fill in the story matrix. Each student or small group of students either selectively or randomly chooses a component from each column as the basis for a new story.

Lesson Objective

The students will

◆ practice problem solving and originality.

Procedures

1. Ask students to help fill in a story matrix by giving the names of four or more books that they have all read. The students generate information about each story's character, location, and action, as well as the emotion felt by a character in order to complete the matrix. Table 5.2 depicts a matrix that is appropriate for the books suggested for this lesson.

Table 5.2. Crazy Stories Matrix

Book	Character	Location	Action	Emotion
Where the Wild Things Are	Max	Wild Things Country	having a rumpus	happiness
Two Bad Ants	ants	in a kitchen	getting too hot	satisfaction
Tacky the Penguin	Tacky	near a frozen ocean	wearing funny clothes	enthusiasm
Fly Away Home	a father	in an airport	watching a bird	sadness

2. Students use one box from each of the categories and list these on their own papers. Suggested methods for gathering student choices include careful selection or random means. When students carefully make a choice from each component, they usually pre-plan possibilities for the story, by playing with how various components could be woven into it. For example, students choosing components from the matrix could think about whether they wanted to write about Max, who got too hot at the airport but was happy he got to go there, or about Tacky, the penguin, who was so sad about being mistaken for a wild thing that all he could do was sit down and talk to a little bird who was also sad.

   Children enjoy using a random method, in which each row of components is numbered. The students roll a number cube to determine which row of each column to use in the story. If a child rolled the numbers 4, 2, 1, 4, they would write a story using a father, a kitchen, having a rumpus, and sadness. (Students simply roll the number cube again if a number appears that is not on the matrix.) The random method makes it much easier for students to get started, although sometimes the resulting stories are not as cohesive as when the careful selection method is used. The random method does, however, seem to incite more creative and original thought from those who are capable.

3. Encourage the students to create a flow chart for their story before initiating any writing. The examples in the second lesson step demonstrated the use of all of the matrix components in one sentence, however, this is not especially desirable for this particular step. Challenge students to elaborate on the components and to build their stories by including additional characters, actions, and other interesting details. Figure 5.2 shows how a flow chart for the random choice 4, 2, 1, 4, involving a father, a kitchen, a rumpus, and sadness might look.

4. Students write their stories as the teacher asks each individual or group questions about the plot, what the character looks like, how the action started, and so forth.

Closure

Students trade stories and become "matrix detectives," who try to figure out all of the matrix components used by the author.

Adults have multiple opportunities to encourage higher-level thinking skills in this lesson.

Fig. 5.2. Caption Story Flow Chart.

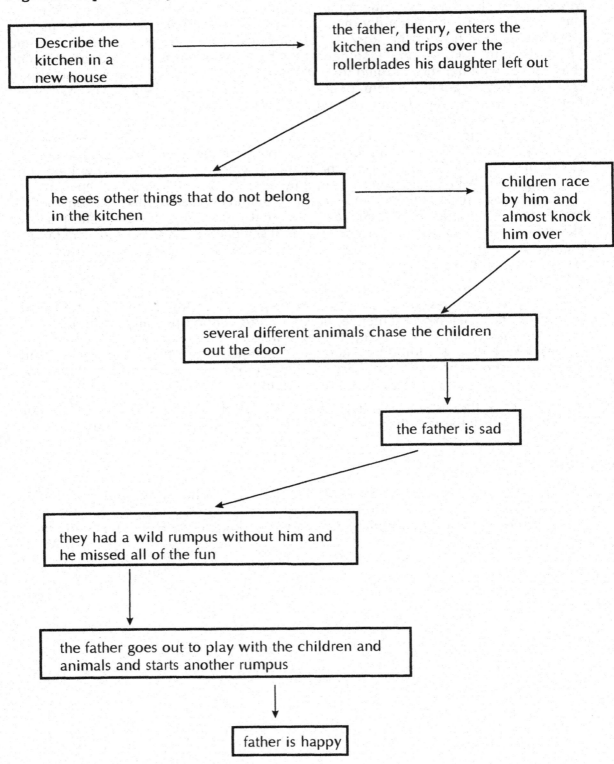

Additional Books in Which Characters Solve Problems

Sweet Clara and the Freedom Quilt by Deborah Hopkinson (1993)

Clara, the young slave in this story, is sent away from her mother before she is 11 years old to work at another plantation. Yet, she clings to her dream of returning to her mother and finding freedom. She works hard learning to become a fine seamstress and eventually earns the chance to sew in the Big House.

Clara is smart and pays close attention to each bit of information she hears about the location of ponds, streams, and other landmarks. When she hears about how the slaves might escape if they had a map, she starts work on one of her own. Clara collects scraps and patches them together to sew a map based on the information she hears. Following the map in her mind, Clara finally escapes. She leaves the quilt behind to direct the journey of others.

This book contains beautiful, clear paintings that capture the essence of the story. Brush strokes are visible in some of the illustrations, and the faces of the characters are impressive. The story is written in black dialect, which helps readers gain a true sense of plantation life.

Sweet Clara and the Freedom Quilt distinctly illustrates the fact that it is not necessary to be scholarly in order to solve problems. Additionally, by sewing her way to freedom, Clara demonstrates that individuals use personal talents to create solutions to problems.

Harry the Dirty Dog by Gene Zion (1956)

The story of Harry was written in 1956; therefore, the illustrations and machines in this book are somewhat outdated. While older children sometimes laugh about this, younger students, kindergarten through second grade, enjoy the story. Harry, a white dog with black spots, enjoys his life, except when he gets a bath. One day, after a good cleaning, Harry hides the scrub brush. Harry's daily adventures include a romp in a pile of coal, which transforms him into a black dog with white spots, and his family cannot recognize him. Harry's problem is how to convince the family that he really is their dog. After many failed solution attempts, Harry digs up the scrub brush, the family gives him a bath, and they finally realize he is their dog.

No Roses for Harry! by Gene Zion (1958)

If students like *Harry the Dirty Dog*, they will probably want to read *No Roses for Harry!* Poor Harry has a different problem in this story, which involves the sweater Grandma knitted for him. His problem resolves itself in an unpredictable manner.

Miss Rumphius by Barbara Cooney (1982)

When the character, Miss Rumphius, was a little girl, her grandfather taught her that she must do three things: go to faraway places, live beside the sea, and make the world more beautiful. She shares her grandfather's many interests and leads a fulfilling life as a librarian who likes to read and travel to interesting places; yet, when she is old, she still has not made the world more beautiful. Finally, with the help of the birds and the wind, Miss Rumphius becomes the Lupine Lady, who spreads seeds over the land that emerge as beautiful flowers. Her solution comes as a quiet "aha," demonstrating to students the value of keeping an open mind and open eyes.

Chapter 6

CHARACTERISTICS OF CREATIVE PEOPLE

Processes discussed in previous chapters—fluency, flexibility, originality, and elaboration—are all part of creative action. They can be improved through training and are especially important in divergent thinking. This chapter provides information about other cognitive and personality characteristics that are common among creative individuals and highly important in the creative process.

Cognitive Characteristics

Tardif and Sternberg (1988) surveyed literature on creativity and developed a chart listing the most commonly mentioned cognitive characteristics of creative people. Few, if any, creative individuals would have all of these traits. The chart Tardif and Sternberg developed after consulting 16 sources by various authors, indicates the number of researchers who referred to each characteristic. The following are those characteristics listed by a minimum of four sources:

- Originality
- Flexible and skilled decision maker
- Articulate and verbally fluent
- Creative in a particular domain

- Metaphorical thinking
- Independent judgments
- Alert to novelty and gaps in knowledge
- Existing knowledge used as base for new ideas (Tardif and Sternberg 1988)

All of these characteristics are explained in various parts of this book or are easily understood, with the exception of the ability to think metaphorically. Metaphors are figures of speech in which one thing is used in the place of another because of their similar characteristics. For instance, the sentence, "John is the Rock of Gibraltar," indicates that John is stable and steadfast just like the rock. Thinking metaphorically allows people to connect their personal experiences to an issue or idea and to create a description in terms of what they understand.

Gordon (1961) promotes this type of thinking and the use of analogies in Synectics, a training technique for developing creative ideas. The processes of Synectics aid people in making connections between seemingly unlike ideas or things in order to gain new insight.

Characteristics of Personality

Characteristics of personality contribute to whether a person will effectively use creative skills and thinking abilities. It is possible for a person to think of highly original solutions to a problem; however, unless the person is willing to take a risk and share those solutions, they may not ever be developed. Characteristics of personality are less easily improved through training than the cognitive characteristics because they are largely affected by personal and environmental factors. No one characteristic alone is enough for creative productivity; a confluence of many characteristics must be present.

Starko (1995) discusses clusters of personality characteristics that are important in creative thinking. These are rephrased below.

Characteristics of Personality

Is willing to take risks

Perseveres, shows drive and task commitment

Exhibits curiosity

Displays openness to experience

Tolerates ambiguity

Has broad interests

Values originality

Exhibits intuition and deep emotions

Is being internally occupied, withdrawn

It is meaningful to students when teachers identify, accept, and nurture these and other characteristics of personality. The characteristics are further described in the information that follows.

Is Willing to Take Risks

Creative students often take risks when they voice original ideas, produce an assignment in a novel format, or suggest unique solutions. This willingness to take risks is important for creative individuals, as well as society. When students think of better, possibly unorthodox ways of doing something, it is uncomfortable for them to simply keep quiet and "go with the flow." Often the ideas have the potential to make significant contributions needed by other people. For example, if every day during center or free time, students fought over who got to work on a favorite puzzle, the teacher or other students would probably suggest a way of taking turns to determine who could work the puzzle. A creative student might suggest simply telling the principal that the class needs two or three more boxes of this puzzle. While the answer sounds absurd since money in schools is always tight, modification of the idea could result in each child bringing a little money to chip in for the puzzle purchase. Perhaps students might think of clever ways to earn class money, such as learning to make paper and selling it for a profit or writing and selling personalized stories in which student clients become superheroes.

Students worried about taking risks sometimes say they cannot do this or that because the teacher will not allow it. They may also discuss concern that the other students will laugh or make fun of them. At times, teachers unknowingly contribute to this by permitting rude students to comment or make facial expressions when others take such risks.

Creative students need help finding other people who share their passion for the unique. They need opportunities to bounce ideas off another person without fear of seeming "weird." *Nimby: An Extraordinary Cloud Who Meets a Remarkable Friend* by Jasper Tomkins (1982), which is described later in this chapter, demonstrates this creative need.

Perseveres, Shows Drive and Task Commitment

Creative students involved in personally meaningful, interesting tasks do not give up easily. They frequently become consumed by a task, working long periods of time, without concern for food or sleep. A creative fourth grade student, who generated a novel idea for making a robot for a futuristic presentation, spent numerous extra hours on the project. He created a dog robot that he could get inside from several boxes, and used a car mechanic's dolly under the boxes so that the creature would roll rather than taking steps to walk. He handled the problem of how to move it by punching two paw holes in the box, covering his hands with brown dog-colored gloves, and extending them to the floor to move the robot. The boy worked continuously on the apparatus until he was satisfied with all of the details. Nothing else seemed to matter during the time he worked on the project.

Exhibits Curiosity

Curiosity is two-sided. Everyone knows what curiosity did to the cat; yet, curiosity and creativity work hand-in-hand. Most people do not just get up in the morning and say, "I'm going to do something creative today." More often, creativity results from sensing a need, wondering about a phenomena, and discovering something new and interesting.

Very young children often require protection from their own curiosity when they attempt to stick paper clips in light sockets and perform other explorations. Teachers note that they watch certain students more carefully than others because their curiosity seems to make them prone to have or cause mishaps. For instance, a middle school boy once heard that the vacant top floor of a building was inhabited by a ghost; so one evening he climbed a nearby tree and threw a rock to tap the window, thinking the ghost would show itself. Naturally, the rock broke the window, and he was in trouble. His curiosity resulted in a broken window.

Curiosity also results in new art forms, entertainment, practical inventions, and additional valuable things. Newton was curious about why an apple fell straight down from a tree rather than sideways or at an angle; this eventually resulted in his theory of gravity (Roberts and Roberts 1995). Curiosity about new ways to express art results in novel costumes, movements, and vocal expression. Curious actors and actresses who wonder about new media of expression and the contribution of unusual costuming to movement on stage might experiment with plain garb covered in mud or some other novel substance. Curious children dig holes on the playground just to see what is down below and crawl in culverts to see what is inside. This natural curiosity, if encouraged, can lead to future productive creative action.

Displays Openness to Experience

Willingness
Come
  I will
  Do you hear it?
   Not yet, but I'm trying
  Listen hard
   I hear, and it's beautiful
  Do you feel it?
   I want to
  Keep trying
    Yes, there, just a touch
  How does it feel?
  Wonderful!

The poem above suggests an exchange between a father and a daughter, during which the girl shows willingness to share Dad's experience. It is presumably more common for people to say, "not now," or "I don't want to," and miss the opportunity for this experience. Creative individuals are open to experience and eager to try new things. This part of their personality helps them learn and gather ideas in a variety of ways and encourages them to view the world from a myriad of angles.

People who are open to experiences try new foods, open their minds to entertainment that is new to them, and listen carefully, rather than critically, to ideas different from their own. They free themselves to use all senses and emotions when absorbing experiences, including crying at movies, genuinely laughing while playing with little children, and expressing anger at indignities.

Tolerates Ambiguity

Starko (1995) states that those who tolerate ambiguity are not discouraged when answers are not clear-cut. They easily adapt when situations give partial information, leaving things incomplete or unsolved. For instance, students enrolled in a university graduate curriculum course were assigned the task of writing a short unit due at the end of the term. The instructor explained that students would work on the unit in class, adding appropriate elements as they were discussed during the term. The students who could tolerate ambiguity ably handled this situation; however, those who could not were uncomfortable much of the term. The latter needed closure and wanted all of the information about the unit to be given initially, in order to be confident that they could master the work. They had considerable difficulty tolerating ambiguity.

Creative ideas occasionally erupt when least expected. Some have stumbled upon an idea or suddenly realized the solution to a problem while taking a shower, going for a walk, or waiting in line at the grocery store. These moments of insight, or "ahas," seldom arrive fully developed and ready for implementation; yet they can spark the flame that fires creative productivity. It is necessary to tolerate the ambiguity or incompleteness of the "aha" in order to gain momentum from it and work out the required details to achieve results. This can, and often does, take considerable time and energy, and the individual must be alert to needed modifications of the original idea.

A third grade boy, inspired by superhero cartoons, decided to write his own series with a character he named Superhound. The boy quickly learned to draw his character but found that writing the series required time and hard work. He tolerated the ambiguity of not having all of the ideas he needed by letting daily experiences influence who the other characters for the series were and what actions they would perform. Grandpa Superhound, with his gray coat and beard, appeared shortly after a Thanksgiving family gathering with grandparents. Almost a year later, the boy still worked on the series and learned to write the cartoon on his personal computer.

Has Broad Interests

Creative students often have multiple interests. Their new experiences entice them to become involved in hobbies and investigations that then lead them to other experiences; and the cycle continues. It is often difficult for students with broad interests to decide what project or topic to explore for an individual school assignment.

Other creative students display interest in a singular domain and invest all of their time in developing skill or knowledge in it. Musicians and dancers typify this type of creative person. It is imperative that teachers understand that many children display creativity in one, dominant area and often cannot think of creative ideas outside this realm.

Values Originality

Another chapter of this book discusses originality in detail; however, valuing originality is somewhat different from producing original ideas and products. Both are important for creative functioning. Those who value creativity recognize it in themselves and others and appreciate uniqueness. These students enjoy hearing novel solutions to problems and think seriously about possibilities offered by others. While other students laugh or ridicule the teacher's idea to dress for their very last day of elementary school similarly to the way they did the first day of kindergarten, those who value originality see the potential for fun in the idea. At times, they piggyback on the ideas to make them more palatable to others.

Older students manifest this characteristic by dressing somewhat differently than others all of the time. This does not mean that they look like the groups of students in their school who dress differently from the majority, but look like each other. Rather, creative student sometimes develop their own unique style of dress.

This characteristic is shown by teachers who do not like to follow the prescribed lessons in their teacher's manuals and make their own unique plans.

Exhibits Intuition and Deep Emotions

Harman and Rheingold (1984) describe intuition as "knowing from within" and Arieti (1976) states, "Intuition appears as a kind of knowledge that is revealed without preparation, or as an immediate method of obtaining knowledge." On occasion, people seem to "just know" things. They have a sense of who will be on the other end of a telephone call before they pick up the receiver, or which idea will be most accepted by the boss. Creative people are open to following their intuition and need opportunities to express beliefs without listing reasons or rationales.

This openness corresponds with sensitivity and deep emotions that should enhance, not stifle, creative production. Skilled listeners detect the difference in a musician who simply plays a piece with technical perfection and one who expresses the soul of the music through the performance. Caring teachers provide the freedom to express emotion appropriately in the classroom and monitor any infringement of personal rights by insensitive students.

Is Internally Occupied, Withdrawn

There are numerous reasons why people want to be by themselves. These include needing silence following an especially frustrating day, wanting to be alone while making a decision, and needing time to organize a plan. None of these involve feeling depressed or unhappy; yet often adults fear the reasons children want to be left alone.

Creative students choose to be alone in order to commit all energy and thought to a creative endeavor. The endeavor takes a life of its own, communicating with an individual through the results of trial and error. It provides all of the stimulation and action a person requires and makes them happy. It is also important to have plenty of time alone to dream and imagine.

Imagination

Adults often think that having a vivid imagination is simply a dimension of childhood that gradually diminishes, and worried parents sometimes wonder when their child will meet "reality." Imagination, however, nourishes creativity by allowing visualization of the possible. Students definitely need to know the difference between reality and fantasy; yet, adults also need to keep imagination in their children alive. Talk to children about their imaginative adventures, encourage them to draw pictures of what they see in their minds, and provide books in which characters have harmless imaginative adventures. A description of two appropriate books, *How I Spent My Summer Vacation* (Teague 1995) and *Judy and the Volcano* (Harris 1994) follows in the lesson portion of this chapter.

Social Skills of Creative Individuals

Some creative children lack the social skills necessary to assimilate with peer groups. Many of the characteristics described in this chapter contribute to unique personalities, causing the child to appear different to peers and some adults. Much of the problem is brought on by the creative student who does not know how to suggest ideas and encourage group work, rather than dominate it. A highly creative third grade boy, who was assigned to a cooperative group to formulate a solution for reduction of the school's large electric bills, provides an example. His group had barely begun discussion when he blurted out his idea. He became so disgruntled when they did not immediately work on his solution that he pulled his chair away from the group and refused to work with them at all.

The parent of an upper elementary student commented to a friend that her daughter felt left out at school. The child was identified as academically gifted and highly creative; therefore she was being pulled out of her regular classroom part of the school day for a special program. The girl wanted to fit in with her peers, and as is typical of early adolescents, it was extremely important for her to feel accepted. The mother had determined that the child did not fit in because she was labeled as gifted and pulled out for the special program. She decided that the girl just wanted to be normal and therefore would not participate in the program any longer. Removing children from a special program does not make them any less creative or gifted and is not an instant cure for being different. Students retain their basic personality characteristics regardless of whether or not they attend special classes.

Torrance (1995) suggests parents and teachers encourage children to maintain the personal characteristics that contribute to their productive creativity, while learning to use personal skills that help them avoid problems with peers and adults. Those who learn the meaning of the word, tact, and apply it to interpersonal encounters may have better luck being accepted.

Two books written by Pat Palmer (1977a and 1977b) provide wisdom and opportunities to discuss concerns about being different. *The Mouse, the Monster and Me* acknowledges that children have a right to be treated fairly and demonstrates what happens when they allow the monster inside to take over their actions. *Liking Myself* shares activities in which students discover that they are valuable and should be happy about who they are. Dr. Palmer writes in words that fourth- and fifth-graders can read to themselves; however, the books are more effective when the teacher shares sections of them with groups of students, who either complete the suggested activities or discuss the content. Sharing the books makes them appropriate for children as young as first grade. These small books are delightfully hand-lettered and illustrated by Betty L. Shondeck and published by Impact Publishers, P.O. Box 1094, San Luis Obispo, CA 93406.

Creativity in Science

Researchers Mansfield and Busse (1981), who studied creativity in science, indicate a slight contrast to the picture of creative individuals painted through description of cognitive and personal characteristics. The researchers investigated personal characteristics, developmental antecedents, and the creative processes used by creative adult scientists. (This chapter will not consider developmental antecedents.)

High intelligence, extensive training, and moderate socio-emotional adjustment are necessary for becoming a professional expert in most fields (Mansfield and Busse 1981). Note, however, that high intelligence is not mandatory for creative thinking. The level of intelligence needed largely depends on the field of study. A person may need to have reasonably high intelligence in order to understand quantum physics; however, intelligence above this level does not automatically cause a person to be more creative in that field. It appears logical that intelligence above the level mandatory for expertise in a field does not correlate with creativity. Interpretation of this for the classroom makes it clear that teachers must encourage creative development among all learners, not solely those who are gifted.

Value of Knowledge

It is obvious that many fields, including science, mathematics, and music, require a great deal of training and the development of a firm knowledge base to facilitate creative production. Highly creative artists with little science background certainly could not be expected to apply creative energy to a scientific problem and produce a valuable solution. The artists probably employ many of the creative processes needed for scientific contribution; however, they lack the required knowledge base. The artists might miss an important discovery simply because they were unprepared to recognize it. Likewise, most creative scientists would probably lack the technical skills and knowledge necessary to produce a great work of art.

Middle school students identified as highly creative, applied the Creative Problem Solving (Parnes 1988) format to a problem posed by a manufacturing company. During the company's manufacturing process, a great deal of visible steam was released out of the plant, and the neighbors thought the company was polluting the air. The students were asked to find a solution to the problem.

Plausible solutions were developed regarding how to convince the neighbors that the steam was not harmful; yet, no effective solutions regarding alternate uses for the steam were developed. The students had numerous ideas about this, but simply lacked the background knowledge to understand what was feasible. If the students had been able to ask specific engineering questions, they might have been able to generate better alternative routes for the steam other than releasing it into the environment.

Mansfield and Busse (1981) comment that professional experts need to have a "minimal level of emotional adjustment." Experts must be psychologically healthy enough to work, and they need enough self-confidence and security to make the required commitment to their own ideas. This is related to the amount of time alone to which most productively creative individuals commit so that their ideas reach fruition. It takes a great deal of fortitude to hold on to and work out an idea that others may have mocked.

In addition to high intelligence, extensive training, and moderate socio-emotional adjustment, professionals in scientific fields have other common personal characteristics:

Personal Characteristics of Scientists
- Autonomy
- Personal flexibility and openness to experience
- Need to be original and novel
- Commitment to work
- Need for professional recognition
- Aesthetic sensitivity

The seeds of many of these characteristics are visible in students and should be nurtured.

Summary

Help students understand the characteristics of creative individuals in order that they can appreciate these attributes in themselves and others. Children often wonder, "Why do I act this way?" yet seldom realize that others have the same question. Help them to see how creative characteristics help people realize their potential.

Fishermen think about the characteristics of fish before they go out on the lake. They realize that different types of fish have various unique traits and habits. The trick is for fishermen to use knowledge of these characteristics to their benefit, and use the appropriate lure and fish in the right spots to make their catch.

RISKING IT ALL

Content: **Art and Social Studies**

Creativity: **Risk-Taking**

Book Selection: Camille and the Sunflowers: A Story About Vincent van Gogh **by Laurence Anholt (1994)**

Anholt based this fictional story on real people and an actual encounter. Students will enjoy reading about the friendship shared by Camille, a young boy, and Vincent van Gogh, the famous impressionist painter. The author-illustrator used pastel watercolors for the visual depiction of the story, which partially counters the book's sad recounting of how townspeople disliked van Gogh. Camille, however, enjoys watching van Gogh work and wishes he had money so he could buy all of his paintings. The story illustrates the ridicule van Gogh endured as he continued to paint in his own original style.

Camille and the Sunflowers has a much happier ending than many of the other books about van Gogh and discusses how the artist's paintings are now worth a great deal of money. While this happily-ever-after ending leaves the reader feeling good about van Gogh, it does not indicate that he endured many more trials in his life. It may be important for teachers to point out that this book represents a short period in van Gogh's life: His life continued to be miserable and his brilliance was not recognized until after his death.

Van Gogh's story is representative of the lives of many artists and musicians whose work is so unique for the time period in which they live that people do not understand or appreciate their brilliance. The book depicts van Gogh's perseverance in the face of external barriers and personal deprivation.

Lesson Capsule

After working in a group and producing unusual drawings, students experience feelings associated with negative comments about their pictures. Discussion of *Camille and the Sunflowers* leads them to an understanding of the perseverance often needed to be creative.

Lesson Objectives

The students will

♦ gain an understanding of people's initial reaction to unique ideas and products,

♦ be able to discuss how to overcome negative statements about ideas and products,

♦ recognize personality characteristics of creative individuals, and

♦ generate examples of perseverance.

Procedures

1. Ask small groups of students to generate highly unique drawings using a technique called "Pass the Picture."

Pass the Picture

A. Students organize into groups of four and move their desks into a rectangle or sit together at a table.

B. Each of the students initiate one drawing by illustrating a simple object or animal on the paper provided. It is extremely important to inform students at this point that their drawings will be changed or "messed up" before they are completed. Some students really get upset when others tamper with their pictures.

C. Students pass their pictures to the right in order that individuals now have another person's initial drawing. These students add something borrowed from another object or animal to the drawing to make it strange and unusual.

D. They again pass the pictures to the right, and another student adds more to the drawing, including a background showing the environment for the strange drawing.

E. Finally, the pictures return to the initial students, who may add any additional marks and color the picture.

F. *Optional:* When using "Pass the Picture" as a stand-alone activity, it is fun to add a fifth person to each student group, who will try to capture the very essence of the picture and give it a clever title. Students then enjoy creating stories describing how the original object or animal became so unique. The following sentences would appropriately initiate a story about how a bear becomes a diving board:

> Momma Bear was completely exhausted after entertaining her young cubs all day by throwing them into the stream.
> Being a very creative mother, Momma Bear decided to borrow an idea she saw once when she wandered a little too close to a human's house.

2. Gather all of the pictures and tell the students they will get them back later. Warn them that their pictures are going to be shared with a very traditional group of adults, and that the students need to be prepared for negative remarks.

3. Later, or on another day, return the drawings to the student groups, reminding them that they probably will not like the adults' comments about their work, but should not take them personally. After all, several different students contributed to each drawing. When returning the drawings, attach a short group of negative comments about each drawing.

4. Ask the original groups of students to discuss how the comments make them feel, and decide whether they would want to do this activity again. Include discussion regarding the term perseverance and how this characteristic could be used in this instance.

5. Read the book, *Camille and the Sunflowers*, prefacing the story with an explanation that one of its main characters has difficulties with his art being accepted, just as the students did.

6. Compare van Gogh's story with the "Pass the Picture" experience. What characteristic does van Gogh display when most people do not like his work? Point out that van Gogh did not try to change people's opinions but simply wanted to continue painting.

Closure

Discuss the loss to society if van Gogh had not persevered. Allow students to share personal episodes of when they have displayed this characteristic or speculate about times they wish they had been as determined as van Gogh.

Related Literature

Van Gogh: The Touch of Yellow by Jacqueline Loumaye (1993)

Fifth grade and older students will enjoy reading this book, or a teacher may want to read it aloud to younger students. The story takes a boy and his uncle on a search to determine if a picture they have was painted by van Gogh. The author uses the pair's excursions as a vehicle for informing readers about the life of the painter. The book contains clear photographs of many of van Gogh's paintings which illustrate points made in the narration. A teacher may want to use the illustrations in this book to supplement lessons.

Degas and the Little Dancer: A Story About Edgar Degas by Laurence Anholt (1996)

Marie wants to become a famous dancer and works diligently when she is accepted into ballet school. There she meets an irritable man who yells at dancers. He is the painter, Edgar Degas, who sketches the dancers, musicians, and teachers at the school. Marie is amazed when she sees some of the sketches that depict the dancers tying their slipper laces, stretching, and doing things other than dancing. When Maria's father becomes ill and she needs money for ballet lessons, Degas offers her money to pose for him. Late one evening when Degas hurries to mold a clay likeness of Marie, she discovers that he is going blind. Although Marie never realizes her dream of becoming a famous dancer, a sculpture of her by Degas later becomes famous. Degas dresses *The Little Dancer* in real clothes and ties a special ribbon in the hair of the sculpture.

This story also depicts a character who perseveres, but in a different manner than van Gogh. Degas fights blindness in order to pursue his creative work and tries to continue drawing through difficult times. Ultimately, his perseverance pays off because he discovers his talent as a sculptor.

BEING DIFFERENT

Content: **Science and Social Studies**
Creativity: **Creative Characteristics**
Book Selection: Tacky the Penguin **by Helen Lester (1988)**

Tacky is a rather odd penguin who does not fit in with his companions. They dive gracefully into the water, while Tacky enjoys doing cannonballs. When the other penguins sing lovely songs, Tacky sings songs with unusual words. Tacky is just different, but it does not seem to bother him. One day, when hunters arrive to capture the penguins, all of the birds run to hide. Tacky, however, stays around to see what is going on, and his strange antics scare the hunters away. Tacky's companions appreciate his efforts and eventually decide that it is not too bad to have an unusual character around.

It is more important to some creative individuals to be their own person than it is to be accepted by peers and society. This does not mean that they do not care about acceptance, but that the need to be creative is more important. Tacky demonstrates this by continuing to be himself, even if the other penguins think that he is different.

While it is highly important to be true to self, it is possible that the important lesson in this story is about others who fail to accept uniqueness. The book illustrates how having someone with a creative personality around can benefit everyone. Students need to learn that appreciating someone or their product does not mean that they have to act like the person or be able to create what the person produces. In fact, it is not even a requirement that they like the person or product.

Tacky exemplifies his true personality, and this is different from individuals who work at being different. Those who try to be different usually have a hidden agenda that may include getting attention, making a statement of independence, or being defiant.

Lesson Capsule

Students experience feelings of "being different" as they make and wear penguin costumes. They reenact the story of *Tacky the Penguin,* demonstrating how the other penguins could be more accepting of Tacky's differences.

Lesson Objectives

The students will

- ◆ appreciate appropriate uniqueness in people,
- ◆ look for meaning behind actions, and
- ◆ recognize personality characteristics of creative individuals.

Procedures

1. Read *Tacky the Penguin* and dramatize part or all of the story.

2. Students can dramatize the story by making simple costumes to help get more into the action. They can make penguin suits from black garbage sacks by slicing holes in the bottom to go over their heads. They may elaborate on this design by cutting the shape of the front white feathers from a white plastic bag and stapling it to the front of the black bag. Students get a better feel for the way a penguin walks if they do not cut arm holes, but keep their arms close to their sides. Tighter bags are also helpful, and larger bags may be altered from the inside with duct tape to create a better fit.

3. The dramatization provides an opportunity for students to experience thoughts and emotions of being different or disliking someone who is different. Discuss these emotions.

4. Ask students to reenact the story by demonstrating ways in which the other penguins could be less critical and more appreciative of Tacky. Make it clear that the other penguins do not need to assume Tacky's characteristics in order to do this.

Closure

Discuss opportunities that the students have in their lives to appreciate creative characteristics.

Personalizing the Lesson

Older or More Able Students

Students make puppets and write a script for the reenactment of Tacky's story. Also, they can replace the penguins with other animals, name one of them, and act out the story. For example, the story line would take a very different direction if Sweetie the skunk was different from the rest of the skunks because she always wore a colorful coat that covered her white stripe.

Younger or Less Able Student

These children may simply dramatize the original book, rather than changing the actions of the other penguins.

Related Literature

Three Cheers for Tacky by Helen Lester (1994)
Tacky's penguin friends worry that he will not be able to learn the cheers well enough to help them win the Penguin Cheering Contest. Tacky characterizes determination and perseverance in this book.

The Emperor Penguin's New Clothes by Janet Perlman (1995)
Perlman's book relates the story of the traditional tale, *The Emperor's New Clothes*; however, she supplies penguins as the characters. The book shows how silly it can be when someone tries to stand out in the crowd for the wrong reasons.

Eggbert: The Slightly Cracked Egg by Tom Ross (1994)
Although Eggbert looks a bit different, he still has a nice talent for painting. He eventually learns to cope with his uniqueness.

Related Literature Selections About Being Different (Characters do not necessarily display creative characteristics.)

Stellaluna by Janell Cannon (1993)
A fruit bat that accidentally falls into a nest is raised by birds in this story. The birds think Stellaluna is odd because she does not like the grasshoppers the mother bird feeds her and tries to sleep hanging upside down. Eventually she has to adopt the birds' habits in order to survive. One day, on a flying adventure, Stellaluna travels too far and becomes lost from the other birds. While hanging by her thumbs, some bats find her and assure her that it is all right to hang by your feet and sleep during the day, because Stellaluna is a bat. Stellaluna shares this new information with her bird friends, and they agree that it is all right for her to be different from them.

This story illustrates that it is usually best to be yourself, even if you act differently than those around you.

An Extraordinary Egg by Leo Lionni (1994)
A frog named Jessica brings home a beautiful large white stone to share with her two friends. The frog friends tell Jessica that the stone is really a chicken egg, and when a creature emerges from the egg, they believe it is a chicken. It does not seem to bother any of the frogs when they learn that the creature enjoys playing with them in the water—a practice uncommon for chickens. One day, while Jessica and the creature are exploring, a bird volunteers to take the so-called chicken to its mother. The frogs think it is very silly when the creature's mother calls it a sweet alligator.

This story not only demonstrates being different, but also proves that things are not always what they seem.

TAKE A RISK

Content: **Social Studies/Cooperation and Survival and Science/Underwater Creatures**

Creativity: **Creative Characteristics—Risk-Taking**

Book Selection: Swimmy **by Leo Lionni (1968)**

A little black fish, Swimmy, lives among numerous little red fish who are highly susceptible to being eaten by larger fish. When Swimmy encounters a school of the red fish hiding in dark shadows, he encourages them to get out and have some fun; but the little red fish are afraid that they will be eaten. Swimmy, a creative fish, solves the problem by showing the school how to work together and form the shape of a large fish in order to swim around the ocean. Swimmy travels with them pretending to be the eye of the large fish.

Lesson Capsule

After brainstorming a list of times when they have been afraid to do something, students analyze this list and choose one or two incidents that would be less scary if others were with them. Students discuss these incidents and talk about how the red fish handled their problem. Students draw pictures depicting opportunities that resulted from the red fish taking a risk.

Lesson Objective

The students will

♦ recognize how cooperation helps in problem solving.

Procedures

1. Students brainstorm a class list of times when they have been afraid to do something. This could include being in kindergarten and afraid to walk to the lunchroom alone, being afraid to answer a class question, or fear of trying a new method for giving a special report.

2. Read the book, *Swimmy,* to the class.

3. Discuss how the idea of "safety in numbers" and creative thinking helped the red fish become brave.

4. Ask students to identify things from their brainstorming list that could be handled through "safety in numbers."

5. Discuss and locate illustrations of the opportunities for exploration and freedom provided the red fish when they took a risk and swam together. Ask small groups of students to draw contrasting pictures of the red fish before and after they took a risk.

Closure

Explain the difference between physical risks and taking a risk in thinking. Discuss opportunities that might be available for students at school to take appropriate risks in thinking.

Personalizing the Lesson

Older or More Able Students

Ask these students to monitor their own thinking for a couple of days and record all of the risks they took and those they did not. This includes thinking about offering a suggestion during class, as well as giving thoughts during writing and on tests. Encourage them, as a group, to develop a list of appropriate risks, in terms of classroom thinking. When should they offer an unusual idea during class discussion and when would this be inappropriate? When should they experiment with a new art form and when should they stay with the media given?

Younger or Less Able Students

The original lesson is appropriate for these students.

Related Literature

The Fantastic Drawings of Danielle by Barbara McClintock (1996)

This beautiful book displays how a young girl's talent and fantasy combine to help her father survive. While her father sells his photographs for a meager income, Danielle visualizes flying frogs and birds in top hats. She cannot seem to paint things as they are even when her father tries to help her. Danielle's creativity and imagination always take over, resulting in fanciful, humorous creatures, for which her father has no use. Ultimately, when Danielle's father becomes ill and she attempts to make photographs to sell, her own creativity allows her to earn an income. A chance encounter with an artist takes Danielle into Madame Beton's studio, where she sees creatures similar to her own. Madame Beton hires Danielle to help her in the studio, and the rest is history.

The Fantastic Drawings of Danielle is a "must read" for all teachers and especially for students who have vivid imaginations.

Daydreamers by Tom Feelings and Eloise Greenfield (1981)

The text of this book quietly mingles with the soft, sensitive illustrations that depict children daydreaming. The black children appear pensive, as the words suggest the power of pausing to imagine and wonder while the rest of the world hurries along. Adults who read this book aloud to children in a slow quiet voice also enjoy the beauty and true meaning of this book.

Minty: A Story of Young Harriet Tubman by Alan Schroeder (1996)

The haunting illustrations produced by Jerry Pinkney tell the story of Minty and the trials she survives on the plantation; but it is Schroeder's narration that truly captures the girl's spirit. The child in this character clearly emerges during a scene in the field where she pretends to be a sunflower that rises to touch the sky. The reader cannot help but root for Minty as she plans to follow the drinking gourd to freedom in the North. Her courage stands out as she learns to swim, read the moss on trees, and follow the stars. The subjugation she wants to escape is documented throughout the story.

This book should take a prominent place in children's literature about slavery. It depicts the perseverance and determination of Harriet Tubman, whose traits evolve in the story while Minty learns to sew, develops a creative plan, and designs an unusual map.

Harriet Tubman was an American abolitionist leader who escaped slavery at about the time the Civil War began. She also helped numerous other slaves run to freedom using the Underground Railroad. Tubman later established a home for elderly African Americans.

"Wanted DEAD or ALIVE": The True Story of Harriet Tubman by Ann McGovern (1965) gives more factual detail of the difficulties Harriet Tubman survived. There are very few pictures in this book; however, an adult could use this book to provide supplemental information.

Follow the Drinking Gourd by Jeanette Winter (1988) provides a nice extension to the story of Minty. It depicts how slaves followed the stars toward a brighter future.

The Art Lesson by Tomie dePaola (1989)

Tommy draws pictures all the time because he wants to be an artist when he grows up. His twin cousins, who are studying to be real artists, tell him that he must practice his art and that he should never copy.

Tommy enjoys the freedom of drawing whatever he wants using any colors he likes; but when he reaches kindergarten, he has a problem. The supplies his teacher provides for painting just do not work very well, and he does not have art lessons in school until first grade. Unfortunately, when he finally reaches first grade, his teacher will not allow him to use his new box of 64 crayons since she wants everyone in the class to use the same eight colors. Tommy becomes even more disgusted about school when the art teacher finally comes to his class and wants him to copy something. He complains, and eventually reaches a compromise with the art teacher, who allows him to draw his own idea after he completes the copying she asks him to do.

Tommy models determination when, as a young child, he states his opinions to adults regarding what he wants and needs. Many creative people, like Tommy, are passionate about their art form and determined to use their own original ideas. Recently, a young, talented painter, who majored in drawing in college, stated that he did not want anyone to "mess with" his unique painting technique. He now successfully sells his original paintings.

Additional Books in Which Characters Display Creative Characteristics

Introducing Mozart by Roland Vernon (1996)

Vernon writes about the composer's life, telling the story from Mozart's birth until his death. The book is well-organized into several two-page sections, clearly titled so that the reader can easily follow the story. The photographs and other illustrations create a colorful expression of the important events in Mozart's life and the history of the period in which he lived. This book is part of a series, which also includes *Introducing Bach, Introducing Beethoven,* and *Introducing Gershwin.*

These books provide background about the pleasant times and tragedies in the lives of each composer. Many characteristics of creative people are displayed throughout the books.

The Frog Who Wanted to Be a Singer by Linda Goss (1996)

A frog who wants to make music can feel pretty sad in a world where only the birds are allowed to sing. Frog's parents support him in his desire to sing; however, his friends make fun of him and call him a fool. Frog finally gets his big break when he convinces Brother Fox to let him be the opening act for the Big Time Weekly concert. Unfortunately, the audience boos Frog off the stage and the Birds come on as customers cheer. All of this makes Frog very frustrated, but he summons his courage, walks back on the stage, and sings into the microphone. When the audience finally hears Frog's boogie woogie beat, they get into the groove and enjoy the crooning. As the book says, that is how rhythm and blues was born.

Frog models original thinking, sensitivity, perseverance, and determination in this book. The story claims that he started the rhythm and blues style of music, which indicates his originality. He also perseveres through difficult times when his friends made fun of him. Frog also displays sensitivity, depicted by his feeling after initial rejections by the audience at the Big Time Weekly concert; and finally shows determination when he returns to the stage.

This delightful book contains wonderful scratchboard illustrations that vividly depict the personality of Frog and the expressions of the other animals. Students enjoy creating their own illustrations using this technique.

Literature Selections in Which Characters Use Their Imagination

How I Spent My Summer Vacation by Mark Teague (1995)

A boy writes his essay, *How I Spent My Summer Vacation*, about a trip he took to visit Aunt Fern. As the boy reads his story to the rest of the class, the book illustrates his narrative as he talks about being captured by cowboys. The narrative is poetic and contains rhyming words that tell about how he became a "first-rate cowhand."

Judy and the Volcano **by Wayne Harris (1994)**

Children often have difficulty starting an essay or an original story, and Judy, the character in this book, is no exception. Judy deals with her teacher, Mrs. Be-the-best-you-can, and another student, Madeline Corsy, who has a good imagination and does well in school. Judy decides that she, too, has great skills and uses her own imagination to turn her story into a wild adventure in which she saves children from a giant iguana and a volcano producing red-hot lava. The delightful ending illustrates Judy and Madeline as they learn they will both read their stories to the school assembly.

Chapter 7

SYNERGY

Tiny creeks and small streams flow slowly across the land, contributing to the growth of the natural environment in their immediate area. When these tributaries meet to form a river, the natural body they create is capable of much more than any single tributary.

Definition and Explanation

Synergy is the plural of synergism, which is "the action of two or more substances, organs, or organisms to achieve an effect of which each is individually incapable" (Webster 1995). Powerful creative synergy results from the synthesis of cognitive and affective factors.

The components of the creative process discussed in this book include fluency, flexibility, originality, and elaboration. Not one of these, alone, yields creative production; however, when they combine, the potential is good. In addition, affective factors of creativity do not automatically yield creative production. This requires some combination of components to even be plausible. The combination of cognitive and affective components creates synergy of mind and spirit, resulting in generative creativity.

A highly fluent individual, who never produces any original ideas, is hardly creative. Highly fluent children in the classroom or home are conceivably annoying at certain times, producing so many possibilities that they cannot get started on anything. Individuals who display skills of elaboration do not necessarily combine these with originality in order that the details they add are interesting or novel. Problem solving, discussed in this book, combines skills of fluency, flexibility, originality and elaboration; yet an individual may lack the personal characteristics necessary to make this successful.

Implementation

The variety of lessons in this book, arranged by chapters, facilitate the development of creative components. Even though a particular lesson may be in the chapter labeled as one creative component, few, if any, of these lessons facilitate the use of only one component. For instance, in Imagination Station, a lesson designed to facilitate the development of elaboration, students figure out a way to create detail on a grid used to diagram a structure they made. While doing this task, students must also think of original ideas regarding a code to represent the elaboration on the grid, such as an "r" to stand for red or a "3" to stand for building a three-story tower.

The lessons are highly valuable; however, readers should not believe that these lessons alone "make" a child creative. When children recognize these skills, as well as their own unique capabilities, as part of the creative process, they receive a license to use them. When all of our homes, schools, and our society legitimize creativity, the world will harvest the benefits.

Simply teaching the lessons in the book is not enough; children must have opportunities to apply the concepts and skills learned. This can be accomplished through the inclusion of creative skills in content-driven lessons, such as those suggested later in this chapter.

Content-Driven Lessons with Creative Components

Many teachers, administrators, and others, during professional workshops or conferences, discuss the need for creativity in schools; however, they often question how adequate time can be allotted for something that is not required. In many cases, teachers note that students spend less time in the regular classroom than ever before, and that they must push hard to teach just the essentials. Haplessly, as teachers feel rushed, students feel hurried, and creative production is impeded.

Parents usually feel caught between their own confounding convictions. All parents are presumably concerned about adequate use of class time and expect their children to learn academic skills necessary for life. Yet, these parents may also value creative thinking and realize the need to nurture it. Parents have power; and they need to articulate the type of classroom balance needed to produce happy, knowledgeable thinkers. It is possible to spend appropriate class time on academics and also promote the development of creative thinking.

The education trend in the late 1990s is conveniently toward a more integrated curriculum, thus setting the table for unique and exciting "dishes" for students. The connections and new understandings that this type of curriculum offers children creates another type of synergy. Teachers who understand how to integrate math and language arts objectives or other subjects should have little difficulty tossing in some spice with creativity objectives. These become a natural part of the daily lesson, without requiring a separate, planned experience that takes valuable class time.

Torrance has suggested introducing some part of creative thinking during a short experience, then following this with required learning that also employs the creative thinking skill. Teachers plan short lessons that introduce components of creative thinking and tools or strategies that aid production. They follow these with lessons built on content objectives in which some portion of the planned activity provides an opportunity for students to use the creative component. For example, students can quickly learn how to use *SCAMPER*, discussed in other chapters, for generating original ideas. Students practice using the technique for finding new ways to use a simple item, such as a pencil. They might think of substituting the pencil for a back scratcher, minifying it for use as a toothpick, or eliminating the point of it and using the eraser end to tickle a baby.

Later, the students are prepared to use *SCAMPER* for generating ideas regarding how to write an original story about the antics of an animal that is part of a unit of study. A class studying Africa could refine writing skills by creating original tales about a lion. The following thoughts result from using the *SCAMPER* technique:

Substitute - substitute the sound of a frog for a lion's roar

Combine - combine the lion's large body with very sensitive emotions that make him cry often

Adapt - adapt the lion's sharp claws by having him wear big soft mittens, so he will not hurt the other animals when he plays with them

Modify, Magnify, Minify - magnify the lion's eyes, so that they make him look very lonely

Put to Other Uses - allow the lion's tail to fan the other animals, instead of himself, in hot weather

Eliminate - eliminate the sharpness from the lion's teeth

Reverse - reverse the way the lion runs so that instead of moving fast, he moves very slowly

With all of these original ideas, an interesting story would certainly be brewing.

It is suggested that, while planning lessons, teachers keep a list of words or phrases that remind them of the creative process. Combine the ideas the words suggest with content or skill objectives in order to give lessons more power.

To be more creative:

- How would you create a different situation?
- Try it a new way.
- Dream.
- What if?
- Where else?
- Be fluent.
- How many different . . . ?
- How would it feel if . . . ?
- Imagine.
- Make an original . . . ?

- How can you take it apart and do something different?
- Give it some detail.
- Could you combine . . . ?
- List the possibilities.
- Play with it.
- How can we solve this problem?
- Look at it from another angle.
- How can you use these things to . . . ?
- Be flexible.

Objectives pertaining to creative thinking are usually embedded in content beyond the basic level of understanding. It appears easier to develop meaningful creative activities that help students apply new learning. For example, students who have developed a basic understanding of nouns and verbs need practice to make their learning meaningful. They can create their own body movements that demonstrate nouns and verbs and simulate sentences for the class. Other students may create specific sounds or use rhythm instruments to indicate when they hear a noun or verb in a sentence. The trick is to let the students decide what they are going to do, rather than the teacher telling them what they are going to do.

Summary

Provide a classroom environment that affords opportunities for creative synergy. This includes ample time for social interaction, discussion in all areas of academics, and free exploration of interests. Synergy does not erupt in a sudden burst of creativity, but rather simmers slowly, waiting for the right classroom elements to blend together and bring it to the boiling point.

Lessons

The suggested lessons that follow do not necessarily use literature selections in which characters exemplify multiple components of creativity; some do not use books at all. Related literature, however, is provided where appropriate.

HARDSHIPS OF EARLY AMERICA

Content: Social Studies—Early Life in America
Creativity: Originality
Book Selection: Teacher's Choice

> **Concepts in Lesson**
>
> People create things to improve lives.
>
> The way people do things changes throughout history.
>
> Learning about history is important to our future.

Lesson Capsule

After learning about early life in America by reading, looking at pictures, or watching a video, students list the problems endured by children in specific situations. Partners then produce sets of before and after drawings, depicting the situation in early America and the same situation in contemporary America. They discuss how thinking creatively was important to inventions, which helped bring about changes and alleviated early problems. There is an optional continuation activity that springboards from this lesson into the future.

Lesson Objectives

The students will

- ◆ recognize problems experienced by children long ago,
- ◆ develop an understanding of the link between needs and creativity, and
- ◆ appreciate the value of original thinking in bringing about change in America.

Procedures

1. Students watch a video about early life in America and look specifically for difficulties experienced by children during this time period. A clip from a television show is often enough to remind students of the era being discussed. Children also learn from stories retold by grandparents about when the children's great-grandparents went to school.

Students may want to talk about children in early America who had to walk long distances to school during inclement weather and sit in one-room schools with little heat. Many find it very unusual that children wrote on slates in school during the early days. Also, they are usually repulsed by the idea of outhouses and wonder about what it would be like to finish recess and be unable to go to the water fountain for a drink. Someone may need to explain what a well is before discussing how to get water from one for a cool drink.

Books also serve the purpose of acquainting children with the past. Consider including adult books that have pictures, as well as fiction and nonfiction children's books. These include *Dandelions*, a picture book by Eve Bunting (1995) about pioneers, and *The Year of the Ranch* (McLerran 1996), which is appropriate for learning about the difficulties of living outside of town.

2. Students make a class list of specific difficulties experienced by children in early America. If students recognize adult problems, discuss how these affected their children. The final list may look similar to the following:

   Difficulties Experienced by Children in Early America
   - walked miles to school
   - wrote on slates in school
   - used outhouses
   - got water from wells
   - were cold indoors in the winter

3. Divide students into groups and ask them to think about why they do not have the same problems that children had in early America. Why don't children in today's schools still write on slates? Why don't they still walk many miles to school? Guide students toward the realization that certain changes and inventions make contemporary life different from that in the early days.

4. Students work in pairs to draw a comparison of children in early America and their contemporaries. Try to get one pair to choose each difficulty written on the original list. One student depicts children long ago in a specific situation, and the other draws a similar situation showing contemporary children. For example, a student draws children walking toward a one-room schoolhouse, and the other draws children arriving at a contemporary school in a bus or car. This creates before and after "snapshots" and prepares students to discuss what happened during the interim between the two time periods. In the school arrival example, the two students should discuss the invention of motorized vehicles that enables modern-day children to ride to school.

Closure

Have students present their drawings and conclusions to the class. Lead them in a discussion of how creativity, specifically in terms of inventions, makes their lives different from children in early America.

Personalizing the Lesson

Older or More Able Students

Rather than providing information about life in early America, ask students to plan how they might gather their own facts. Suggest that they conduct interviews with older people, during which the student would inquire about situations that the adult's parents talked about.

When feasible, encourage students to interview adults who grew up in other countries. What experiences were common to all people during a specific period in history? The use of international e-mail so that children can share information, may be possible in some schools.

Younger or Less Able Students

Some students have a more difficult time figuring out the inventions that helped solve many of the problems in early America. If this occurs, provide pictures of many different inventions, including those that were helpful in alleviating the difficulties on the children's list. Let the children choose the picture of the invention that corresponds to each problem.

Rough drawings of the inventions, some of which may be located in coloring books and others in clip art collections, may be created. The author usually makes a rather crude drawing and labels it with the appropriate name so the students will know what it is.

Extension

1. Piggyback on the above lesson by continuing it on another day, when children are encouraged to consider the present day. Ask students to brainstorm a list of problems or situations that contemporary children would like to change.

    Make it clear that students are not just telling their own problems but are presenting general problems that many children encounter. Some children think about not having the "right" pair of shoes or having to wear hand-me-down clothing. Other students think about problems, such as a house being too small for the family, having to share a room with siblings, not getting to see friends who live across town, and so on. Watch out! Children may try to turn this into a gripe session. An example list follows:

    ### Things Contemporary Children Would Like to Change
    - sharing a bedroom
    - sharing a TV with adults
    - wearing hand-me-down clothes
    - having to ride the bus to school
    - not getting to stay up late to watch a favorite television show

2. Ask students to look 50 years into the future and visualize tomorrow's children. It is quite helpful to take children on a fictitious journey into the future. Consider using the following scenario:

All of us are eagerly boarding the vessel, not knowing quite what to expect. Inside there are comfortable, soft, inviting chairs, one for each of us, in our own favorite color. When we sit in the chairs, they slowly begin to mold to just the right position, and we are more comfortable than we have ever been. Music surrounds us as the vessel begins to move on its voyage into our future, and we look into the best of what it can be. As we look out the windows, cloud-like whiteness floats by, then fades, and clears. We see children in their yards, at home, in school, and other places, but it seems that things have changed. Life for them is not the way is was for us, and it appears that the things we wanted to change are now different. Look closely at the children and let's keep this picture in our minds as the windows of our vessel once again become clouded. Before we know it, our comfortable chairs seem to be nudging us to get up, and, when the doors of the vessel open, we know we must leave; however, we will not forget.

3. Discuss any changes the students observed that will solve the problems they wrote on their original list. Discuss what will have to occur between now and the future in order that the difficulties are solved. Would any new inventions help? If so, what are they, and who will build them?

Closure

Students share or write what they want to do to contribute to the future.

THE "BOARD" GAME

Lesson Capsule

Who is supposed to solve the problems of the day? We count on the Board of Education, the Administrative Board, the Board of Directors, and sometimes the "bored." In this game, each "Board" has a chance to create the answers to problems, such as how to make a swing for an ant and how to measure time. Children work in teams, using an odd collection of things to make a product designated by a task card. They earn specific wages for each suitably completed task.

Lesson Objectives

The students will

♦ practice risk-taking,

♦ examine problems from a new perspective,

♦ practice cooperating with team members, and

♦ use divergent thinking skills.

Materials Needed

A. Task cards with designated dollar values

create a swing for an ant	$10
make something with which you can tell time	$10
make a toy for a cat	$ 8
create a seasonal decoration	$10
make a chair for a doll	$12
player's choice: make up your own task	$ 7
make a device for keeping someone cool	$ 8
make something for keeping the sun out of your eyes	$10
create a noise maker	$ 9
create some sort of game	$12
make a face decoration (must stay on by itself)	$ 7
design and make a decoration for the top of a cake	$ 7
make something that is mobile or moves without help	$10
make a decorated key holder (to carry or put on wall)	$ 8

Teachers developing a theme choose tasks that correspond to the topic. For instance, in order for the game to encompass the theme, Pioneer Life, simply advise students that the products are to be used by pioneer children.

B. Materials Choices for Teams

Every team receives the following supplies:

- two paper clips
- a 15-inch piece of string
- tape
- scissors

Each team may also choose any five of the following:

- paper plates
- paper cups
- feathers
- pencils
- kitchen items (wooden spoons, wire whisks, can openers, and so on)
- socks
- shoelaces
- a belt
- sticks
- other interesting items

Optional "Board" Rooms

Students use folders placed vertically on desks, room dividers, or cardboard to make their own board room, so others cannot see what they are making.

Procedures

1. *Components of Creativity:* fluency, flexibility, originality, problem solving

   Small teams of three or four students either create the name of their "Board" or choose a card that indicates the name. Suggestions include Board of Bicycles, Board of Rock Musicians, Board of Soccer Players, Board of Cool, "Bored of School." A class studying a specific topic, such as pioneers, can be directed to choose names accordingly. Pioneer topic "Boards" could include Board of Wagons, Board of Wheel Makers, Board of Scouts, and so on.

   Write the names of the "boards" on a chart similar to Table 7.1.

Table 7.1. Board Game Chart

Segment	Board of Mathematicians	Board of Recyclers	Board of Readers	Board of Environmentalists
1				
2				
3				
Total $				

2. *Components of Creativity:* acceptance finding, a stage of problem solving

   Each team chooses five more supplies from those provided, the number of which is designated by the teacher, and receives those additional items allotted for every team. Be sure that children know they do not need to use every supply for what they are making. Students are often confused about this and make the task more difficult than necessary. (Students may take apart a completed product in order to reuse supplies for the next one.) Prior to starting the game, the teacher determines the number of tasks teams attempt. This is largely based on amount of time dedicated to the game and the age or attention span of the children.

Rules of the Game

1. Solutions to task cards must be free-standing or hanging.

2. Each game segment consists of eight minutes, during which teams may complete a task.

3. Team members must remain in their board area for the entire eight-minute segment.

4. Teams that cannot resolve their differences of opinion will be disqualified from a segment.

3. *Personal Characteristics:* communicating and cooperating

    A member of each group blindly picks a task card and reads it. The teams begin work on the task by discussing it and formulating a plan before transforming any items.

4. *Critical Thinking Skills:* analysis, evaluation; *Personal Characteristics:* appreciation of originality

    After eight minutes, teams stop working, read their task card to the entire group, and demonstrate the product developed. The other team members and the teacher evaluate whether the product satisfies the task and award the dollar amount designated on the task card.

5. The teacher or a designated child recorder keeps track of the dollars earned on a chart. (See Table 7.2 for a sample tally.)

Table 7.2. Wages Earned by Boards

Segment	Board of Mathematicians	Board of Recyclers	Board of Readers	Board of Environmentalists
1	$10	$0-disqualified	$10	$12
2	$10	$12	$12	$ 7
3				
Total $				

6. The game is over after the predetermined number of segments. Totaling the earnings for each team brings closure to the game; however the purpose is to practice problem solving, not to declare a winner. Do not allow students to make winning the goal.

Personalizing the Game

Older or More Able Students

Teams of players take pleasure in writing task cards. Teachers need to monitor this activity and check the cards for appropriateness. Teams that know that they may receive some of their own cards during the game tend to write more sensible tasks than those that think they are giving them all to some other group.

Younger or Less Able Students
(including those who find it difficult to be creative)

Activity 1. Make the game guidelines more flexible for younger students by giving the teams sacks of supplies and asking them to create a minimum number of purposeful products from the supplies given. Ask students to tell the name of their products and what tasks they fulfill.

Activity 2. Adults can make simple items, such as a basket out of a foam cup and a pipe cleaner, and young students will delight in trying the items. At times, while the child is reproducing the adult's product, he or she adds something new to it. Simple reproduction does not require creative thinking unless something is being changed; this part of the activity merely sets the stage for later creativity. Do not tell the children they are being creative when they are reproducing something but point out that if they add to it they are thinking creatively.

It is simpler for them to reproduce an item that they can see and touch; however, using a photograph or diagram of the item makes the process challenging. For example, an adult or older child creates a swing for a small doll by tying a piece of string at each end of a stick. The younger child reproduces the swing using the same objects, then attempts to create a swing from other objects provided. These include pipe cleaners, a paper cup, a feather, a cotton ball, and a pencil. These steps guide those who have difficulty thinking of creative ideas or adapting materials for specific purposes.

HOLIDAY HANNAH

Content: **Social Studies and Language Arts**
Creativity: **Flexibility, Originality, Elaboration**
Book Selection: **Choose According to Holiday**

Although no child has ever seen Holiday Hannah, she visits classrooms all over the country. The children know when she has been in their room because she leaves special templates for the children to use in making pictures. The templates are made out of poster board and are a variety of different shapes depending upon the holiday. For instance, in one classroom Holiday Hannah left the templates of a bunny's tail and ear and an egg the week before Easter. The ear and tail must have come from a big bunny because the tail was about four inches wide and the ear was six inches high. The students found them with a note from Hannah attached.

> Dear Children,
> I've left you a few things that you can use in your drawings. Just trace around one of them and see what kind of a picture you can make. I'll be looking for your pictures the next time I come by your room. Have fun with them.
> Yours truly,
> Holiday Hannah

Lesson Capsule

Holiday Hannah leaves holiday shapes in the classroom, and the children turn them into pictures.

Lesson Objectives

The students will

♦ use art as a medium for expression, and

♦ practice being flexible, original, and elaborate.

Procedures

1. Encourage students to look at the shape templates from several different angles before deciding what they will draw. It is often best if this is an individual activity in which the children are not seated with others working on similar pictures. It seems that once young children have seen the shape used a certain way, they want to do the same thing. Older children have less trouble with this.

2. Provide children with large sheets of plain paper and crayons or markers.

3. Encourage them to add a background or other features to make their initial drawings more elaborate.

Chapter 8

LET'S TALK

Teachers and Parents

Teachers and parents have many things in common and both hope that children will become healthy, happy, productive members of society. No matter who is responsible for the children, the youngsters arrive with basically the same needs; therefore, this chapter makes little distinction between how parents or teachers nurture children.

Although articles and book chapters, such as this one, often begin with descriptions that help adults determine whether children are creative, this is not important here. While it is not essential to identify creativity, it is essential to nurture it; therefore, assume that the child or children have the potential for creativity.

Very young children are naturally creative as demonstrated through their insatiable curiosity and drive. Follow a two- or three-year-old around for a day, and this will be clear. Typically, little children look at, smell, touch, and sometimes taste things, like a flower in the yard or other objects, learning all they can from the experience. They look in ditches, use rocks to dig in the dirt, talk to inanimate objects, and experiment with all sorts of things. These children unknowingly take risks, tolerate ambiguities, and make original analogies, such as calling a newspaper tossed through the air an airplane. The natural process of creative learning occurs as children explore and wonder. The question is, What can adults do to protect and nurture natural creativity?

Consider the following three main areas through which adults influence children:

Personal Behaviors of Adults
Words and Actions Used by Adults
Opportunities for Development Provided by Adults

Personal Behaviors of Adults

Value Creativity

Do adults value creativity? Many people pay lip service to creativity when asked this question; however, they may not desire to be creative or to encourage it in their children. It is vital that adults working with children learn about creativity and its value to society. Information in many of the chapters of this book explains the contributions creative individuals have made and suggests other reading that is available. Adults and children do not need to be personally highly creative in order to appreciate and value uniqueness; yet, it is difficult for adults to nurture creativity in children when they do not understand its power. Make it a goal to discover creativity and model it whenever possible.

It is also wise to learn as much as possible about the characteristics of creative individuals, some of which were discussed earlier in this book. Look anew at these by contemplating the many joys creative children bring to adults. Additionally, adults should anticipate the possible problems that can arise when dealing with creative children. Often adults cannot prevent a problem; however, understanding the reasons for the difficulty can help remedy its effect. Table 8.1 provides information on the joys and problems of dealing with creativity.

Exercise caution with children who claim that their behavior results from being creative. Even though a student may think that creating an artistic rendering of the principal on the bathroom wall is a unique project, the act is still wrong and must be dealt with appropriately. Some children step outside the boundaries of creative thinking and exercise deviant behavior. Adults have to provide the training that encourages children to develop positive values that help prevent wrongdoings.

Model Effective Communication

Adults who model effective communication set the stage for children to reciprocate and become articulate about needs and goals. It is sometimes hard to believe how much children listen to adult conversations, but spending a short time listening to children at play brings this point home. During playtime, adults hear young children pretending to be adults. (Luckily, teachers seem to take some secret oath that bars them from repeating these incidents to someone else.) Children need to hear adults setting agendas for the next day or week, making long-term plans, and agreeing to disagree.

Table 8.1. Personality Characteristics of Creative Individuals and Their Concomitant Joys and Problems

Characteristic	Joys	Problems
Is willing to take risks	tries new things	does things that hurt themselves or others
Perseveres, shows drive and task commitment	will stick with something until it comes to fruition	ignores important things while working on a single project
Exhibits curiosity	shares the fun of exploring things and learning	irritates others by asking too many questions
Is open to experiences	sees possibilities in experiences	wants to try too many things
Tolerates ambiguity	remains open and continues to think when solutions or ideas take a long time to form	resists closure to the point of irritating others who are ready to proceed to something new
Has broad interests	knows much about many things and shows interest in what others know about	cannot settle down to one thing and therefore never becomes expert
Values originality	admires originality in many things	likes and wears unusual clothing and enjoys friends who do not fit the norm
Exhibits intuition and deep emotions	has a good feel for situations and necessary actions; is appropriately sensitive	shows emotion in front of peers who do not understand it
Is internally occupied, withdrawn	can enjoy being alone and find things to do	does not share inner thoughts; appears to be daydreaming when adults need focused attention

Like Yourself

It is quite healthy for people to like themselves. This contributes to a positive self-concept, provides self-confidence, and makes life more enjoyable. For one reason or another, many people spend a good deal of time degrading themselves. Statements like, "My hair is ugly, I don't know why I can't just wear a wig," and "I'm so stupid. I should have remembered to do that. I'm really dumb today," do not do much for a healthy self-image. Children easily pick up this attitude and often downgrade themselves or their peers. Teachers and parents need to be careful to show respect for each other during conversations. Children at school often repeat what is said in the home about the teacher and vice versa.

Words and Actions Used by Adults

Timing

Help children learn that timing is essential when sharing creative ideas or products. Adults who have just completed a difficult day at work and driven home in heavy traffic do not necessarily enjoy creative jokes the minute they get home. Teachers who normally appreciate and invite creative ideas do not want to hear them during a serious class discussion on a topic, such as safety. Teach children that in order to exercise suitable timing, it helps to take the audience's perspective before sharing ideas.

Timing and tact go hand in hand, and many children have considerable difficulty with the latter. The use of tact helps children when they are unsure whether their timing is "off." In cases of creativity, the use of tact involves being able to share creative thinking without offending others. Note that tact is also essential during the acceptance finding stage of Creative Problem Solving.

Rewards

People are either intrinsically or extrinsically motivated, and adults are usually skilled in offering the latter to children. A five dollar bill for an A on a report card, a trip to the ice cream store for a good behavior day at school, and other gestures seemingly offer children attainable goals that are sometimes necessary. It is, however, intrinsic motivation that most positively correlates with creativity. Part of that intrinsic, or internal, motivation comes from the enjoyment of a task or exploration. This joy often fades as children think about extrinsic, or external, prizes for their work. The focus suddenly shifts from doing a great job and enjoying the work to earning the reward.

What types of extrinsic rewards or external motivations pop up at home and school? Some of these are subtle but have the same effect as tangible rewards. Readers have probably heard some of the following comments:

- No, you can't have three dollars for a C. We only pay for grades of A.
- If you will hurry up and finish that drawing, the whole class can go out early to recess.
- I want you to write the best story you can so that it will have a chance to win the contest.
- This project must include a nice display board, because your parents will see it at open house.
- If you will get all those drawings and models off your floor, we'll have time to go for ice cream.
- Let's see if you can do as well as your sister, who never had any trouble in math.

Some of the above comments are appropriate in certain situations; however, they are not suitable when trying to encourage creative thinking.

Competition can be detrimental to creative production when children win, receive praise, and then feel that they must continue to be the best. Although some adults do their best not to emphasize winning, children sometimes place unnecessary pressure on themselves, then develop strategies to relieve the stress. For example, a long distance runner who used creative thinking to plan his strategy for a race he won, may later opt not to give 100 percent in the next race. If he does not give full effort, then he has an excuse for not winning.

Suggest that children relate the intrinsic reasons for continuing a project. These probably include the following:

This is really fun to work on.

I didn't even know I could do this. I might actually be good at it!

This is cool. I don't think anyone else has ever thought of it before.

I like working on this. I can forget everything else that is going on and concentrate. I wish I could do this all the time.

Legitimize these feelings in order that children learn the appropriateness of working for personal satisfaction. Help them find interests that are intrinsically satisfying, as opposed to providing tangible rewards for creative thinking.

Emma's Rug by Allen Say (1996) illustrates this point in a story about a little girl who wins many prizes for her artwork. Emma displays no interest in the ribbons, trophies, and plaques that fill her room. She believes her inspiration comes from a small rug she received at birth; however, after winning competitions, she hides the rug in a drawer. One day her mother washes the rug and Emma feels that since the rug has changed she has no more ideas for her work. The story eventually illustrates that motivation, inspiration, and imagination come from within the child rather than from some other source such as the rug. Allen Say truly captures the essence of Emma's feelings in his illustrations of facial expressions. Even the smallest child will be particularly touched by the anguish on Emma's face when she learns that her rug has been washed. This book sets the stage for a good discussion of motivation and competition.

The Magic Boots by Scott Emerson and Howard Post (1994) is another selection about inspiration and imagination. This book chronicles a boy's imaginary adventures that take him many places. The boy associates his adventures with his boots that he thinks are magic; therefore, trouble begins when the boy's feet start growing too big for the boots. His attempts to make his feet fit the boots add humorous elaboration to the story. Eventually, he realizes that the magic is his and did not come from the boots.

Fact and Fantasy, Constructive and Destructive

Children must, obviously, recognize the difference between fantasy and reality, and luckily, this generally happens during normal growth and development. If imaginative thought encroaches on sense and reason, children find themselves in trouble. At times, children injure themselves while pretending to be superheroes or escape artists. There are far too many true stories about children who did not realize they were holding a real gun or know that the knife they were playing with did not bend like the one they saw in a cartoon. Adults must endeavor to keep children safe, yet allow them to retain vivid imaginations.

The book, *Tugford Wanted to Be Bad* by Audrey Wood (1983), illustrates an instance of trouble-making by an imaginative child and a sensible response by adults.

Tugford Wanted to Be Bad by Audrey Wood (1983)

Tugford, a little mouse, takes pretending to the extreme in this book, when he tries to be a real outlaw. He actually steals something from his parents and buries his treasure. An interesting turn of events helps Tugford realize it is better to just pretend. The mouse parents demonstrate the need for adults to monitor children's activities and to make sure that young people understand the boundary between pretending and reality. This knowledge does not have to thwart creativity.

Vivid imaginations parallel creative thought, enabling people to visualize something contrary to reality. Help children recognize the continuum from reality into fantasy, noting that both extremes are important for productive creative behavior. Knowledge from past and current realities leads toward the envisioning of future improvement. Seeing the possible leads to positive action.

Opportunities for Development Offered by Adults

Knowledge and Expertise

Parents informally provide opportunities for students to use creative thinking at home. For instance, creative thinking results from using a "Guess what I just learned?" format and following this at a separate time by saying, "Let's try what I learned." The scenario that follows helps clarify this suggestion:

Component Introduction

Adult: I learned the neatest thing today. I read that if you are trying to create a really good way to do something, it's a good idea to try to think of lots of ideas before you decide on one. I always just take the first idea that pops in my head, but next time I'm going to try this out. It's probably still O.K. if I use the first idea, but at least I will give my other thoughts a chance.

Child: We do that sometimes at school and the teacher writes our ideas on the board.

Adult: This way of thinking is called fluency.

Child: We just call it brainstorming.

Later Component Usage

Adult: What do you have for homework tonight?

Child: Nothing.

Adult: Don't you have some kind of report or project due?

Child: That isn't due until the day after tomorrow.

Adult: Let's talk a little about it today, so at least you will know what you're going to do. What are you supposed to prepare?

Child: It's a short report about tornadoes that we have to give in front of the class. We turn in the report. I'm just going to look it up in the encyclopedia. It won't take long.

Adult: Why don't we use that new thing we talked about. You called it brainstorming, and I said it was fluency. I wonder how many other ways you could get information for your report.

Child: I know; I could watch television all evening and see if there's a show about tornadoes!

Adult: That's a great idea, but I don't see any "tornado" specials listed. What else could you do to collect information?

Child: I could look in other kinds of books or link into that new computer at the library. It has discs with all sorts of information.

Adult: What else could you do on the computer?

Child: Oh, I forgot. I could "surf the net" like they talk about on that television commercial, or what is that mail stuff you do? Is it e-mail? I wonder if I could get anything that way.

Adult: You have some great ideas. Can you think of anything else? What are you trying to find out with e-mail?

Child: I want to know if someone out there has ever actually been in a tornado. Oops, I already know someone like that. What about Aunt Mildred? Didn't the roof on her house fly away in Oklahoma?

Adult: Yes, but how could you get information from her before the report is due.

Child: Dial collect!

Adults also help children gain the benefits of gathering their own information through exploration, trial and error, and observation of phenomena. Think about learning as an adult. Does the most joy and understanding come from information another person told you or from information derived by exploring, experimenting, and digging deeply into a subject? Which is easier to recall? Adults provide motivation for children when they organize opportunities for individual or group discovery.

Once children express interests, adults must listen carefully to their discussion and questions of the topic. What do they actually want to do or learn? Suggest ways in which they may find the answers; please do not simply tell them the answer. If possible, provide opportunities for hands-on experience or observation of important parts of the topic. For instance, children interested in snakes may actually have a great desire to visit one and to hold it. Trips to the library to see pictures and read about the creatures probably will not be enough. Often adults must swallow their own inhibitions and dislikes in order to facilitate children's learning.

People spend hundreds of dollars on children who say they want to play musical instruments. For example, it is reasonably common to spend two or three thousand dollars on an instrument and lessons for the child who said he wanted to play the piano. Problems arise about six months later when the child says he has learned enough and will not be studying piano anymore. Parents scream; the child cries; the piano teacher feels sad; and the family has a beautiful piece of furniture that no one can play. The problem largely stems from the child who did not say exactly what he wanted to do and the parents who did not listen carefully and probe the subject. The boy really just wanted to perform in the school talent show and thought he could quickly learn to play something on the piano. He did not want to play the instrument forever! The author apologizes to all piano teachers for this example, which merely illustrates what can happen when adults do not find out the real reason for a child's request.

The other side of the piano problem springs forth when a child yearns to play an instrument for no obvious reason other than the sheer joy of it. Most expertise in the field of music requires extensive training that costs more than any child's allowance. However, musical creativity cannot emerge unless the adults can manage to arrange training for the child.

Children also need help from adults in order to use creative thinking in other areas. If interested in "saving the whales," children must form a working knowledge of information about what the animals need in order to survive. Additionally, they must understand the environment and issues surrounding the cause before they can produce valuable creative solutions. In most cases, it takes willing adults to help children acquire this knowledge. It would be interesting to know the number of missed opportunities for great discoveries resulting from the lack of knowledge to recognize them.

Safe Risks

When can children afford to take risks? Many children do not foresee the possible effects of their risk-taking, while others dwell on them. In both situations (as presented below), children benefit from opportunities to explore a risk-free environment.

Jan wanted to suggest a novel idea for the end of the year party, but she was afraid that the other kids would call it "dumb," and that her teacher would not like it. Jan would rather keep quiet than risk ridicule. On the other hand, Joe also had a great idea for the party that included making silly hats and parading through the middle school halls. Instead of merely contributing this idea to the class discussion, Joe made a goofy looking hat, dressed weirdly, and paraded through the halls of the elementary school. He never had a clue that the other students, classroom teachers, and principal would not be thrilled with his idea. Both Jan and Joe need guidance to know when and how to take a risk. Adults furnish this by providing safe times when children's ideas are respected by the family or classroom peers.

Choices

Children who have opportunities to make choices tend to be more motivated (Amabile 1989), and motivation affects creativity. Adults should consider whether they can accept children's choices before offering them. Children tend to distrust those who offer and then take away opportunities. Teachers have ample opportunities to help students learn to make good choices, such as providing a selection of project topics, offering a menu of math activities to fulfill a requirement, and allowing students to help select curriculum units. Occasionally, parents let children choose things, like where they will eat and what television show to watch. Respect these choices.

Time Alone

There is a difference between being alone and being lonely; children and adults keeping a constant pace of school, lessons, games, work, and so on, find little time to be alone to think. Children need to get to know themselves, and this happens when they think, dream, and relax. Freedom from conversation, television, and music (although some find this helpful) allows the mind to settle itself, calms the body, and opens avenues for creative thought. Many highly creative children find their own solace, spending large amounts of time in their rooms, alone outdoors, or other places. Parents who question this find it reassuring to learn why children need to be alone. It is also helpful for adults to arrange their own private time to survey personal thoughts. The children might just have the right idea! Spending time alone facilitates the development of autonomy, and adults can be available to help children, without hovering.

Teachers support children's need for private time when they have students reflect on an experience or a reading. An exhausted teacher could have students write about their field trip after they return to the classroom. Students can be amazingly quiet while they write and may truly enjoy this reflection. Teachers should also provide reflection time after students work on skills and concepts. This allows the children to process what they have learned and to integrate it with their existing knowledge and understanding. Horizontal enrichment of concepts naturally provides the time students need to personalize information and skills.

Safe Space

Creative children tend to have lots of "stuff" that they work with, which they do not want stored. Often, this is both visually annoying to the rest of the family or class, as well as hazardous to passersby. Children work diligently on a project and then move on to explore something else before the initial task is completed. Adults worry that these children will never finish anything and are learning bad habits; occasionally, this is true, but it is not a given. Children may leave a project because they are not ready to conclude it, they have not decided what to do next, or because another interest pulls them away. Adults cannot force children to reach closure to creative thinking. This is the opposite of leading a horse to water but being unable to make it drink; adults can make children dismantle or put away their "stuff" but cannot make them stop thinking about their projects.

A creative young college student recently stated that children should have many low, empty shelves in their rooms for storing their tools and materials. She also suggested low shelving with cabinet-like doors, so that the implements of creativity can be locked away from siblings.

Friends

All children need friends who understand their plans and dreams and accept their differences. Some adults drive hours from home so that a child may visit with others who share the same interest. Children sometimes associate with friends older and younger than them, simply because of something they enjoy doing together. For instance, a twelve-year-old child may play with seven- or eight-year-olds who live nearby because the older child still wants to play make-believe. Or, a younger child may enjoy the company of an older friend who has a vast knowledge of dinosaurs. Attempt to learn why a child wants to visit with another in order to determine if the relationship is healthy. The story about a creative cloud, *Nimby: An Extraordinary Cloud Who Meets a Remarkable Friend* by Jasper Tomkins (1982), discussed on page 94 in the chapter about characteristics, depicts the need for friendship and the fact that people find friends where they least expect them. Nimby eventually makes friends with a creative island.

Literature for Conceptual Understanding

Adults use good children's literature as horizontal enrichment, to both initiate and enrich conceptual understanding. All of the following children's books present the concept of friendship and/or helping others. They also contain other concepts that allow these books to be used with various themes. Adults should continue to reinforce the importance of friendship, even though this is not the lesson theme. For example, *Miss Tizzy* (Gray 1993) and *Peach and Blue* (Kilborne 1994) are obviously selections about friendship and fit nicely with this conceptual theme.

The Wind Garden (McAllister and Fletcher 1994) depicts the concept of the elderly and the young benefiting from time together. Students may be studying the elderly; however, friendship is also an important concept.

Sam Johnson and the Blue Ribbon Quilt (Ernst 1983) deals with gender issues and whether men can or should do quilting. Teachers often use this book during a mathematics lesson to build the concept of patterning or geometric shapes. Friendship again emerges from this story and enriches children's understanding of the concept.

Smoky Night (Bunting 1994) deals not only with multicultural issues, but also with contemporary violence. This book illustrates a different side of friendship.

Nurture Creativity

"Children will be children," and the creative and potentially creative arrive at the home or classroom door quiet, sensitive, loudly obnoxious, or curiously questioning. The trick is to care about their creativity, nurture their thinking, and help them become all that is possible.

Resource Books and Articles for Parents and Teachers

Amabile, Teresa. 1989. *Growing up creative: Nurturing a lifetime of creativity.* New York: Crown.

Dr. Amabile is an authority in the psychology of creativity, who writes clearly about the phenomenon and about motivation. Important points in the book suggest how adult efforts to encourage creativity often result in destroying it. Amabile includes numerous activities and techniques that parents may use to enliven creativity at home. Her succinct definition of creativity and suggestions on how to recognize it prepares readers to acknowledge creativity in children.

de Bono, Edward. 1992. *Teach your child how to think.* New York: Viking.

De Bono discusses his views regarding the critical nature of thinking and offers numerous tools to help children and adults think in new ways. These include Six Thinking Hats; Consider All Factors; Consequence and Sequel; and Alternatives, Possibilities, Choices. The concepts of these tools are appropriate for all ages, including five-year-olds; however instruction in their use may be more appropriate for second-graders and older. *Six Thinking Hats* does, however, work well in the kindergarten classroom. The tools discussed in the book were originally developed for adults, particularly those in business and industry; yet, they are also highly useful with students. Adults who read this book should reap benefits for their own thinking, as well as learning to help children.

Meador, Karen. 1992. Emerging rainbows: A review of the literature on creativity in preschoolers. *Journal for the Education of the Gifted* 15(2): 163–81.

This article is for those who are seriously interested in learning more about the results of research on creativity in early childhood.

Meador, Karen. 1993. Parent to parent, surviving early childhood with a creative child. *Gifted Child Today* 16(2): 57–59.

The author uses anecdotes from early days with her own children as examples of manifestations of creativity. The article also includes information and suggestions for parents or teachers of young creative children. This selection is also mentioned in the chapter on characteristics.

Palmer, Pat. 1977. *Liking myself.* San Luis Obispo, CA: Impact Publishers.

Palmer, Pat. 1977. *The mouse, the monster and me.* San Luis Obispo, CA: Impact Publishers.

These two selections are mentioned on page 99 in the chapter about characteristics, and both provide interesting reading and activities for home or school. Although they are not written specifically for creative children, both help open communication lines between children and adults regarding emotions and sensitivities. *The Mouse, the Monster and Me* encourages children to speak up for themselves without becoming a monster who alienates others. *Liking Myself* helps children learn more about themselves. Children enjoy the hand lettering by Betty Shondeck in both books. They may be ordered directly from Impact Publishers, P.O. Box 1094, San Luis Obispo, CA 93406.

Saunders, Jacqulyn. 1986. *Bringing out the best: A resource guide for parents of young gifted children.* Minneapolis, MN: Free Spirit Publishing.

Many people consider creativity to be a marvelous form of giftedness. Whether or not parents follow this line of thinking, *Bringing out the Best*, offers useful advice. Part I of this book specifically discusses giftedness and, among other topics, suggests how to tell if a child is gifted. Although Part II also discusses giftedness, the solid information is important for parents who are interested in brain development, activities to do with children at home, and the selection of toys. Saunders, in the third section of the book, talks about how to choose a preschool, which is obviously intended for parents of very young children.

Summary

Everyone needs a contemporary who is striving to improve the lives of children and appreciates the value of facilitating creative development. It is important to share and compare ideas and concerns with others, as well as joys and "ahas," in order for adults to know if a child's actions are creative. Adults should share both incidental creative happenings and planned activities or excursions that nurture children's creative development.

Additionally, small groups of creative children enjoy getting together to work on a project, learn about something of interest, or just talk about their own experiences. Creative people generate sparks that ignite not only their own ideas but also those of others. Seize opportunities to build a fire.

AFTERWORD

The deed is done
The task complete
Tonight, I hope
I'll surely sleep

Yes, writing has
been quite a chore
My husband says
"You'll write No More!"

But as I type
these final pages
I realize they will
keep for ages

And though I'm weary
the time's been spent
in searching to
my heart's content

to find the lessons
that we all need
to help the children
to succeed

So if you find
that you can choose
lessons to clear
those classroom blues

Your children will
then help you see
that they've been waiting
long for these

You'll learn real fast
that creativity's needed
and to my words
you will have heeded

The life and blood and
the future of man
you are holding
in your hand

Teach your children to value creativity, help them strive to learn how to use its power, and always allow them to believe they can lasso the moon.

Karen S. Meador, 1997

REFERENCES

Ackerman, Karen. 1988. *Song and dance man.* New York: Alfred A. Knopf.

Aiken, Conrad. 1977. *Who's zoo of mild animals.* New York: Atheneum.

Allard, Harry, and James Marshall. 1977. *Miss Nelson is missing!* Boston: Houghton Mifflin.

Amabile, Teresa. 1989. *Growing up creative: Nurturing a lifetime of creativity.* New York: Crown.

Anaya, Rudolfo. 1995. *The farolitos of Christmas.* New York: Hyperion Books for Children.

Anholt, Laurence. 1994. *Camille and the sunflowers: A story about Vincent van Gogh.* Hauppauge, NY: Barron's Educational Series.

———. 1996. *Degas and the little dancer: A story about Edgar Degas.* Hauppauge, NY: Barron's Educational Series.

Arieti, Silvano. 1976. *Creativity: The magic synthesis.* New York: Basic Books.

Bunting, Eve. 1991. *Fly away home.* New York: Clarion Books.

———. 1993. *Someday a tree.* New York: Clarion Books.

———. 1994. *Smoky night.* New York: Harcourt Brace.

———. 1995. *Dandelions.* New York: Harcourt Brace.

Buscaglia, Leo. 1982. *The fall of Freddie the leaf.* Thorofare, NJ: Charles B. Stack.

Cannon, Janell. 1993. *Stellaluna.* San Diego, CA: Harcourt Brace Jovanovich.

Carle, Eric. 1973. *I see a song.* New York: Scholastic.

———. 1996. *Little cloud.* New York: Philomel.

Charbonneau, Manon, and Barbara Reider. 1995. *The integrated elementary classroom: A developmental model of education for the 21st century.* Boston: Allyn & Bacon.

Cleary, Beverly. 1986. *Two dog biscuits.* New York: William Morrow.

Cooney, Barbara. 1982. *Miss Rumphius.* New York: Puffin Books.

Cummings, Pat, ed. 1992. *Talking with artists.* New York: Bradbury Press.

Davis, Gary, and Sylvia Rimm. 1994. *Education of the gifted and talented.* 3d ed. Boston: Allyn & Bacon.

de Bono, Edward. 1985. *Six thinking hats.* Boston: Little, Brown.

———. 1991. *Six thinking hats for schools: 3-5 resource book.* Logan, IA: Perfection Learning Corporation.

———. 1992. *Teach your child how to think.* New York: Viking.

Deedy, Carmen Agra. 1993. *Tree man*. Atlanta, GA: Peachtree.

———. 1994. *The library dragon*. Atlanta, GA: Peachtree.

———. 1995. *The last dance*. Atlanta, GA: Peachtree.

dePaola, Tomie. 1983. *The legend of the bluebonnet*. New York: G. P. Putnam's Sons.

———. 1989. *The art lesson*. New York: G. P. Putnam's Sons.

Diller, Harriett. 1996. *Big band sound*. Honesdale, PA: Boyds Mills Press.

Eberle, Robert F. 1990. *SCAMPER: Games for imagination development*. Buffalo, NY: D.O.K. Publishers.

Emerson, Scott, and Howard Post. 1994. *The magic boots*. Salt Lake City, UT: Gibbs Smith Publisher.

Ernst, Lisa Campbell. 1983. *Sam Johnson and the blue ribbon quilt*. New York: Lothrop, Lee & Shepard.

Feelings, Tom, and Eloise Greenfield. 1981. *Daydreamers*. New York: Dial Books for Young Readers.

Flournoy, Valerie. 1985. *The patchwork quilt*. New York: Dial Books for Young Readers.

Fontenot, Mary Alice. 1983. *Clovis Crawfish and the orphan Zo-Zo*. Gretna, LA: Pelican Publishing.

Gackenbach, Dick. 1996. *Barker's crime*. New York: Harcourt, Brace.

Gag, Wanda. 1941. *Nothing at all*. New York: Coward-McCann.

Galdone, Paul. 1975. *The gingerbread boy*. New York: Houghton Mifflin/Clarion Books.

Gardner, Howard. 1983. *Frames of mind: The theory of multiple intelligences*. New York: Basic Books.

Goodrum, Don. 1992. *Lettres Acadiennes: A cajun ABC*. Gretna, LA: Pelican Publishing.

Gordon, W. J. J. 1961. *Synectics: The development of creative capacity*. New York: Harper & Row.

———. 1974. Some source material in discovery-by-analogy. *The Journal of Creative Behavior* 8(4): 295–300.

Goss, Linda. 1996. *The frog who wanted to be a singer*. New York: Orchard.

Gray, Libba M. 1993. *Miss Tizzy*. New York: Simon & Schuster.

Harman, Willis, and Howard Rheingold. 1984. *Higher creativity: Liberating the unconscious for breakthrough insights*. New York: G. P. Putnam's Sons.

Harris, Wayne. 1994. *Judy and the volcano*. New York: Scholastic.

Heide, Florence Parry, and Judith Heide Gilliland. 1992. *Sami and the time of the troubles*. New York: Clarion Books.

Hest, Amy. 1986. *The purple coat*. New York: Four Winds Press.

Hopkinson, Deborah. 1993. *Sweet Clara and the freedom quilt*. New York: Alfred A. Knopf.

Howard, Jane R. 1985. *When I'm sleepy*. New York: E. P. Dutton.

Isaksen, Scott, Brian Dorval, and Don Treffinger. 1996. Brainstorming. *THINK* (December): 11–14.

Jacobs, Heidi Hayes, ed. 1989. *Interdisciplinary curriculum: Design and implementation.* Alexandria, VA: Virginia Association for Supervision and Curriculum Development.

Jacobs, Howard, ed. 1973. *Cajun night before Christmas by "Trosclair."* Gretna, LA: Pelican Publishing.

Kilborne, Sarah. 1994. *Peach and Blue.* New York: Alfred A. Knopf.

Laden, Nina. 1994. *The night I followed the dog.* San Francisco, CA: Chronicle Books.

Lasky, Kathryn. 1995. *She's wearing a dead bird on her head!* New York: Hyperion Books for Children.

Lester, Helen. 1988. *Tacky the penguin.* Boston: Houghton Mifflin.

———. 1994. *Three cheers for Tacky.* Boston: Houghton Mifflin.

Levine, Ellen. 1995. *The tree that would not die.* New York: Scholastic.

Lionni, Leo. 1968. *Swimmy.* New York: Pantheon Books.

———. 1994. *An extraordinary egg.* New York: Alfred A. Knopf.

Loumaye, Jacqueline. 1993. *Van Gogh: The touch of yellow.* Art for children series. New York: Chelsea House.

Macaulay, David. 1988. *The way things work: From levers to laser, cars to computers—A visual guide to the world of machines.* Boston: Houghton Mifflin.

MacLachlan, Patricia. 1994. *All the places to love.* New York: HarperCollins.

Maker, C. June, and Aleene Nielson. 1996. *Curriculum development and teaching strategies for gifted learners.* Austin, TX: Pro-Ed.

Mansfield, Richard S., and Thomas V. Busse. 1981. *The psychology of creativity and discovery: Scientists and their work.* Chicago, IL: Nelson-Hall.

McAllister, Angela, and Claire Fletcher. 1994. *The wind garden.* New York: Lothrop, Lee & Shepard.

McClintock, Barbara. 1996. *The fantastic drawings of Danielle.* Boston: Houghton Mifflin.

McCloskey, Robert. 1941. *Make way for ducklings.* New York: Viking.

McGovern, Ann. 1965. *"Wanted dead or alive": The true story of Harriet Tubman.* New York: Scholastic.

McLerran, Alice. 1991. *Roxaboxen.* New York: Puffin Books.

———. 1996. *The year of the ranch.* New York: Viking.

Meador, Karen. 1992a. The effect of synectics training on gifted and nongifted kindergarten students. Ph.D. diss. Texas Woman's University.

———. 1992b. Emerging rainbows: A review of the literature on creativity in preschoolers. *Journal for the Education of the Gifted* 15(2): 163–81.

———. 1993. Parent to parent, surviving early childhood with a creative child. *Gifted Child Today* 16(2): 57–59.

———. 1994. The effect of synectics training on gifted and nongifted kindergarten students. *Journal for the Education of the Gifted* 18(1): 55–73.

———. 1996. SCAMPER: Putting fun into idea generation. *THINK* (December): 15–17.

Micklethwait, Lucy. 1993. *A child's book of art: Great pictures, first words.* New York: Dorling Kindersley.

———. 1996. *A child's book of play in art: Great pictures, great fun.* New York: Dorling Kindersley.

Oppenheim, Joanne, and Barbara Reid. 1968. *Have you seen birds?* New York: Young Scott Books.

Osborn, Alex F. 1963. *Applied imagination.* 3d rev. ed. New York: Charles Scribner's Sons.

Osofsky, Audrey. 1992. *Dreamcatcher.* New York: Orchard.

Otto, Carolyn. 1996. *What color is camouflage?* New York: HarperCollins.

Palmer, Pat. 1977a. *The mouse, the monster and me.* San Luis Obispo, CA: Impact Publishers.

———. 1977b. *Liking myself.* San Luis Obispo, CA: Impact Publishers.

Parnes, Sidney. 1988. *Visionizing.* East Aurora, NY: D.O.K. Publishers.

Perlman, Janet. 1995. *The Emperor Penguin's new clothes.* New York: Viking.

Piirto, Jane. 1992. *Understanding those who create.* Dayton, OH: Ohio Psychological Press.

Polacco, Patricia. 1996. *Aunt Chip and the great Triple Creek dam affair.* New York: Philomel.

Politi, Leo. 1948. *Song of the swallows.* New York: Aladdin Books, Macmillan.

Puccio, Kristin, Susan Keller-Mathers, and Don Treffinger. 1997. *Adventures in real problem solving: Facilitating creative problem solving with primary students.* Sarasota, FL: Center for Creative Learning.

Riecken, Ted J., and Michelle R. Miller. 1990. Introduce children to problem solving and decision making by using children's literature. *The Social Studies* (March/April): 59–64.

Roberts, R. M., and J. Roberts. 1995. *Lucky science: Accidental discoveries from gravity to velcro, with experiments.* New York: John Wiley.

Rogers, Carl. 1961. *On becoming a person: A therapist's view of psychotherapy.* Boston: Houghton Mifflin.

Ross, Tom. 1994. *Eggbert: The slightly cracked egg.* New York: Putnam.

Roukes, Nicholas. 1982. *Art synectics: Stimulating creativity in art.* Worcester, MA: Davis Publications.

Sandler, Martin. 1996. *Inventors: A Library of Congress book.* New York: HarperCollins.

Saunders, Jacqulyn. 1986. *Bringing out the best: A resource guide for parents of young gifted children.* Minneapolis, MN: Free Spirit Publishing.

Say, Allen. 1991. *Tree of cranes.* Boston: Houghton Mifflin.

———. 1996. *Emma's rug.* Boston: Houghton Mifflin.

Schick, Eleanor. 1992. *I have another language, the language is dance.* New York: Macmillan.

Schotter, Roni. 1996. *Dreamland.* New York: Orchard.

Schroeder, Alan. 1996. *Minty: A story of young Harriet Tubman.* New York: Dial Books for Young Readers.

Scieszka, Jon. 1992. *The stinky cheese man: And other fairly stupid tales.* New York: Viking.

Sendak, Maurice. 1963. *Where the wild things are.* New York: Harper & Row.

Shaw, Charles G. 1947. *It looked like spilt milk.* New York: Harper & Row.

Silverstein, Shel. 1964. *The giving tree.* New York: Harper & Row.

Sirett, Dawn, ed. 1996. *The really amazing animal book.* London: Dorling Kindersley.

Soto, Gary. 1996. *Chato's kitchen.* New York: G. P. Putnam's Sons.

Stanley, Diane. 1996. *Leonardo da Vinci.* New York: Morrow Junior Books.

Starko, Alane. 1995. *Creativity in the classroom: Schools of curious delight.* White Plains, NY: Longman.

Stepien, William, Shelagh Gallagher, and David Workman. 1993. Problem-based learning for traditional and interdisciplinary classrooms. *Journal for the Education of the Gifted* 16(4): 338–57.

Stevens, Janet. 1995. *Tops and bottoms.* San Diego, CA: Harcourt Brace.

Swartz, Robert J., and D. N. Perkins. 1990. *Teaching thinking: Issues and approaches.* Pacific Grove, CA: Midwest Publications.

Tardif, Twila, and Robert Sternberg. 1988. What do we know about creativity? In *The nature of creativity: Contemporary psychological perspectives.* Edited by Robert Sternberg. Cambridge, MA: Press Syndicate of the University of Cambridge.

Teague, Mark. 1995. *How I spent my summer vacation.* New York: Crown.

Thiele, Colin. 1986. *Farmer Schultz's ducks.* New York: Harper & Row.

Tomkins, Jasper. 1982. *Nimby: An extraordinary cloud who meets a remarkable friend.* San Diego, CA: Green Tiger Press.

Torrance, E. Paul. 1979. *The search for satori and creativity.* Buffalo, NY: Creative Education Foundation.

———. 1994. *Creativity: Just wanting to know.* Pretoria, South Africa: Benedic Books.

———. 1995. *Why fly?* Norwood, NJ: Ablex Publishing.

Treffinger, Donald J. 1994. *The real problem solving handbook.* Sarasota, FL: Center for Creative Learning.

Treffinger, Donald J., and Carole Nassab. 1996. Strategies and tools for thinking. *THINK* (December): 3–6.

Turvey, Peter. 1992. *Inventions: Inventors and ingenious ideas*. Danbury, CT: Franklin Watts.

United Nations. 1995. *My wish for tomorrow: Words and pictures from children around the world*. New York: Tambourine Books, William Morrow.

Van Allsburg, Chris. 1988. *Two bad ants*. Boston: Houghton Mifflin.

Vernon, Roland. 1996. *Introducing Mozart*. Parsippany, NJ: Silver Burdett.

West, David, and Steve Parker. 1995. *53½ things that changed the world and some that didn't*. Brookfield, CT: Millbrook Press.

Wheatley, Nadia, and Donna Rawlins. 1989. *My place*. Brooklyn, NY: Kane/Miller.

White, Linda. 1996. *Too many pumpkins*. New York: Holiday House.

Winter, Jeanette. 1988. *Follow the drinking gourd*. New York: Dragonfly Books, Alfred A. Knopf.

Wood, Audrey. 1983. *Tugford wanted to be bad*. New York: Harcourt Brace.

———. 1985. *King Bidgood's in the bathtub*. New York: Harcourt Brace Jovanovich.

Wood, Audrey, and Don Wood. 1994. *The tickleoctopus*. San Diego, CA: Harcourt Brace & Co.

Woodruff, Elvira. 1991. *The wing shop*. New York: Holiday House.

Yamaka, Sara. 1995. *The gift of Driscoll Lipscomb*. New York: Simon & Schuster.

Yolen, Jane. 1974. *The boy who had wings*. New York: Thomas Y. Crowell.

———. 1996. *Sky scrape/city scape: Poems of city life*. Illustrated by Ken Condon. Honesdale, PA: Wordsong/Boyds Mills Press.

Yorinks, Arthur. 1990. *Ugh*. New York: Michael di Capua Books.

Zion, Gene. 1956. *Harry the dirty dog*. New York: Harper & Row.

———. 1958. *No roses for Harry!* New York: Harper & Row.

Zolotow, Charlotte. 1995. *When the wind stops*. New York: HarperCollins.

AUTHOR/TITLE INDEX

SUBJECT INDEX

ABOUT THE AUTHOR

Karen Meador enjoys studying, writing about, and sharing children's picture books. She collects her favorites and uses them with children, in consulting, and in university classes. Dr. Meador has taught courses in children's literature, creativity, early childhood education, elementary education, and gifted and talented education at various colleges and universities. She prides herself on a creative presentation style and the ability to train teachers to encourage thinking among their students.

Dr. Meador has also been a teacher in first, second, and third grades and has taught piano to all ages. She has also served kindergarten through fourth grade students in a gifted resource room. She worked with middle school students for several summers at the Louisiana Creative Scholars' Program and taught preschool music in early childhood centers. Her past field-based teaching and current consulting work allow her to maintain her connections with teachers and their students. Dr. Meador states, "I cannot write about children unless I seize every opportunity to be inside their classrooms, their learning centers, and their young minds."

Dr. Meador lives in San Marcos, Texas, with her husband Don. They are building a home on their property, Dreamcatcher Ranch, and hope their two grown children will come to visit.

From **Teacher Ideas Press**

FROM THE LAND OF ENCHANTMENT: Creative Teaching with Fairy Tales
Jerry D. Flack

Inspiring and practical, this book offers a wealth of ideas, curriculum, resources, and teaching techniques that promote multiple intelligences, critical thinking, and creative problem solving, all through the common theme of fairy tales! **All Levels**.
Gifted Treasury series; Jerry D. Flack, Ed.
ca. 230p. 8½x11 paper ISBN 1-56308-540-2

CRITICAL SQUARES: Games of Critical Thinking and Understanding
Shari Tishman and Albert Andrade

Developed through Project Zero at the Harvard School of Education, these simple but powerful games are designed to develop students' critical-thinking skills and deepen their understanding of topics they are already studying. **Grades 3–12**.
xv, 123p. 8½x11 paper ISBN 1-56308-490-2

TalentEd: Strategies for Developing the Talent in Every Learner
Jerry D. Flack

"The best little resource for classroom teachers!" according to *Teaching K–8*, this book shows how all children can learn well and achieve excellence if provided with opportunity and challenge. Activities promote literacy, integrated learning, diversity, and academic excellence. **Grades K–12**.
Gifted Treasury Series; Jerry D. Flack, Ed.
xiii, 249p. 8½x11 paper ISBN 1-56308-127-X

FIFTY FABULOUS FABLES: Beginning Readers Theatre
Suzanne I. Barchers

Involve young children in reading and learning with these charming readers theatre scripts based on traditional fables from around the world. Each has been evaluated with the Flesch-Kincaid Readability Scale and includes guidelines and tips for presentation, props, and delivery. **Grades 1–4**.
ca. 130p. 8½x11 paper ISBN 1-56308-553-4

LITERATURE LINKS TO PHONICS: A Balanced Approach
Karen Morrow Durica

Integrate phonics skills and high-frequency word recognition with reading of authentic texts. Common phonetic generalizations and an annotated bibliography of books that can be used to teach phonetic elements are included in the book. It also has a list of high-frequency words and a section of suggested independent follow-up activities. **Grades K–3**.
xiv, 149p. 8½x11 paper ISBN 1-56308-353-1

BOOKWEBS: A Brainstorm of Ideas for the Primary Classroom
Barbara LeCroy and Bonnie Holder

Here is an organized framework for children's literature integration. Featuring book titles and themes that appeal to young children, it combines literature-based applications with stimulating ideas and activities to use as springboards for learning. **Grades 1–3**.
xi, 193p. 8½x11 paper ISBN 1-56308-109-1

For a FREE catalog or to place an order, please contact:

Teacher Ideas Press
Dept. B54 · P.O. Box 6633 · Englewood, CO 80155-6633
1-800-237-6124, ext. 1 · Fax: 303-220-8843 · E-mail: lu-books@lu.com

Check out the TIP Web site!
www.lu.com/tip

CPSIA information can be obtained at www.ICGtesting.com
Printed in the USA
LVOW03s0906130915

453967LV00029B/425/P